The Smallest Spark

The Smallest Spark

A World Set Ablaze
by a Little Life and a Little Way

JOHN D. WRIGHT

authorHOUSE®

AuthorHouse™
1663 Liberty Drive
Bloomington, IN 47403
www.authorhouse.com
Phone: 1 (800) 839-8640

Published by AuthorHouse   03/14/2016

ISBN: 978-1-5049-5184-5 (sc)
ISBN: 978-1-5049-5088-6 (hc)
ISBN: 978-1-5049-5183-8 (e)

Library of Congress Control Number: 2015915610

Print information available on the last page.

*In loving memory of my mother who first introduced
me to Thérèse. May she rest in peace.*

Based on various works concerning the life of St. Thérèse of Lisieux:

Execution of Pranzini, published by *The New York Times*, August 31, 1887.
The Story of a Soul---Autobiography of St. Thérèse of Lisieux, 3rd Edition
Therese (sic.) *and Lisieux*---Pierre Descouvemont and Helmuth Nils Loose
St. *Therese* (sic.) *of Lisieux: Her Last Conversations*---Trans. by John Clarke, O.C.D.
Thérèse of Lisieux and Marie of the Trinity---Pierre Descouvemont; trans. Alexandra Plettenberg-Serban
The Passion of Thérèse of Lisieux---Guy Gaucher
Maurice & Thérèse: The Story of a Love---Patrick Ahern
My Sister St. Thérèse---Sister Genevieve of the Holy Face (Celine Martin)
The Plays of St. Thérèse of Lisieux---Sister Cécile of the Carmel of Lisieux, Msgr. Guy Gaucher, O.C.D., et al., eds.; trans. Susan Conroy and David J. Dwyer
The Prayers of Saint Thérèse of Lisieux---Sister Cécile of the Carmel of Lisieux, Msgr. Guy Gaucher, O.C.D., et al., eds.; trans. Aletheia Kane, O.C.D.
St. Thérèse Doctor of the Little Way---Franciscan Friars of the Immaculate, eds.
Letters of St. Therese (sic.) *of Lisieux Volume I*---Trans. by John Clarke, O.C.D.

Introduction

This work covers the life of Marie-Françoise-Thérèse Martin (a.k.a. Saint Thérèse of Lisieux or the Little Flower) from her teenaged years until her death at age twenty-four from tuberculosis, with some aftermath. Also included are appendixes that contain an updated version of a lecture that I have presented on Thérèse to different audiences, which includes selected quotes from Church documents relating to Thérèse's canonization and being made a Doctor of the Church, and a reference guide for works on her that may or may not have inspired some of the scenes that I have written into this story.

Thérèse lived in Lisieux in France's lower Normandy in the late 1800's. She was a woman who intended never to be known and, viewed only on the surface, should never have been known, and yet is a Saint and Doctor of the Catholic Church, who is known to Catholics and non-Catholics alike---or so I have read. Sadly, at least on a personal level, I find myself encountering people who have never heard of her, and if they have, then their knowledge is only superficial, since they have not gone beyond the stereotypical floweriness often attributed to her, and so are unable to see just how valuable knowing her life can be in finding meaning in one's own life.

She is also known, thanks to Pope Pius XI who canonized her, as the Greatest Saint of Modern Times. According to Pope John Paul II, her autobiography, *Story of a Soul*, and other works pertaining to her have had a profound positive impact not only on the Catholic Church but also on Protestants and non-Christians. In other words, there seems to be something for everyone, regardless of background, when it comes to Thérèse.

Why is this so? How does a girl who enters a cloistered convent (meaning she was willingly cut off from the outside world) at the age of fifteen and ends up dying at twenty four, totally unknown to the world, and barely known by many of the religious sisters with whom she lived, end up being canonized a saint just over two decades later, and, on top of that, declared a Doctor of the Church?

It all started with what would seem like chance circumstance and simple obedience. The circumstance was that Thérèse had older biological sisters who lived in the convent with her and the act of obedience was for her to write about her life and her relationship with God, something she never would have done if she had not been told to by her superiors in the convent.

The work, which came to be known as *The Story of a Soul*, was never intended to be published. It was merely going to be a memento for her convent and especially her biological family living within its walls. Yet it became one of the most beloved works of literature in the world.

In my opinion, the attribute that has drawn so many to love Thérèse over the many years, since her death in 1897, is her bold confidence which she began tapping into at an early age. This confidence is not to be confused with arrogance, and it does not mean she always felt certain about what she was doing, or that she never suffered. She knew it was not going to be easy to be allowed to enter a Carmelite monastery at age fifteen, and the task of appealing to certain people to bring this about, such as Pope Leo XIII, must have seemed daunting. After entering, while still a teenager, her community was hit by a flu epidemic, and she was one of the few left standing who had to attend to all of the sick. She was also tasked, at an earlier than normal age, with aiding in the instruction of incoming novices. Thérèse saw these things through faithfully, though they seemed bigger than her.

Her confidence really shined, ironically, when she was hit with tuberculosis in 1896, which, eighteen months later, brought about her death. The disease caused tremendous physical suffering. In the midst of that she also experienced a sense of abandonment. Everything she grew up believing in suddenly felt like a lie. To summarize that, she was not only experiencing outer physical suffering, but also internal emotional and spiritual suffering. Yet the confidence she held onto caused many in her community to not even believe she was sick, much less experiencing spiritual darkness.

Thérèse's confidence also clung to a belief that any suffering that we experience, no matter how apparently trivial or devastating, can be used for good. It is a confidence that has touched many people and helped them to find a sense of meaning and direction in their lives that they might not have otherwise known.

The following pages attempt to retell her story, with reference to her autobiography and many other works that have been written about her, in the hopes that readers will be inspired to personally look at these works and discover Thérèse for themselves.

"But now we know the praises of this pillar, which glowing fire ignites for God's honor, a fire into many flames divided, yet never dimmed by sharing of its light…"

---The Exsultet

Prologue

Late Nineteenth Century France...

It is a quiet night in the Rue Montaigne, as an old mistress chats with her maidservant, Annette, while her twelve-year-old daughter sits on the floor nearby, playing with her doll. They are suddenly interrupted as Henri Pranzini, a bearded man wearing a short rounded top-hat and overcoat, kicks open the door to their house and proceeds in, brandishing a pointed butcher knife. Annette grabs her daughter and pushes her to her mistress who frantically ushers the panicked little girl, still clutching her doll, into a back room and locks the door, leaving the girl's mother alone as Pranzini approaches her with a stoic and unfeeling look on his face.

Knowing that she is all that stands between this madman and her daughter, Annette snatches a pot off of the nearby stove and attempts to attack him. In an almost singular motion, Pranzini catches her arm as his knife goes into her stomach. She emits a shocked gasp as the pot slips out of her hand and clangs on the wooden floor. Still clutching Annette's arm, Pranzini withdrawals the knife and turns her around, as she crumples to her knees. Pranzini pulls her head back by her hair and his emotions remain unchanged as he takes the knife to her throat. After Annette's gasping ceases, Pranzini lets her fall to the floor, walks past her body, and kicks open the door to the back room as Annette's child and her mistress scream.

And God wept...

Part I

Beginnings

Chapter 1

Celine...

What is our world coming to? I just heard the news about a man who killed two women and a twelve-year-old girl. He slit their throats! The little girl was almost decapitated! What kind of monster does that!? At least they caught the guy. He'll be dead soon. Not that it will make the world a better place, but that's how it works. These are my thoughts as I walk home.

I step into my house and it seems too quiet. Usually my little sister, Thérèse, runs to the door to greet me. I go into our dining room and see her sitting at the table looking cute as always with her long blonde hair let down and wearing a pretty white dress. She doesn't look up at me when I walk in. Her emerald eyes are staring off as if in a trance. I then notice what she's looking at: a newspaper. *No way!*

She doesn't flinch as I snatch the paper off of the table. I try to get her to snap out of her trance as I fold up the paper and sit down beside her.

"Thérèse! You know Papa doesn't want you reading the newspaper, you're too young!"

She's unfazed, doesn't even look at me, and seems to change the subject.

"Celine...would you have a mass said for my intentions?"

"What?"

Thérèse looks at me and smiles.

"I need a mass said for my intentions."

Now I'm curious. I lean close to her and lower my voice.

"What intentions?"

Thérèse lays her face on the table, reaches up and begins playing with my hair.

"You'll laugh."

I know what will get her to open up. I smile and kiss her on the cheek. Works every time.

"Come now."

She gives in.

"It seems Pranzini will die unrepentant. I do not want him to fall into hell."

I was afraid that's what she was reading about. I don't know whether to be edified or disturbed by such earnest concern for a coldblooded killer. I try to make sense of it.

"You care for him in spite of the fact that he murdered two women and a little girl younger than you?" I guess a soul's a soul, though. I'll play along. "Do you think we can convert him?"

She smiles at me again as she stands up with her hand still in my hair and laughs.

"Have a mass said for my intentions!"

Chapter 2

Pranzini sits in his cell waiting for what is to come. He's telling himself that he couldn't care less. *Can we just get it over with?*

He looks up as his cell door is opened and is surprised to see a priest walk in and sit down in front of him.

"Self-righteous pig. Come to tell me that God's wrath will soon be upon me?"

The priest smiles gently at Pranzini.

"No. I have come to tell you that though society will soon take its vengeance upon you, nevertheless, God's mercy awaits you. I am here to invite you to embrace it."

Almost out of reflex, Pranzini spits in his face and hisses through his teeth. "I AM INNOCENT!" He cocks his head with mocking smile. "What of you...PRIEST?"

The priest makes no protest as he wipes the spit off of his face with a handkerchief. He simply looks again at Pranzini and smiles, nodding his head.

Two guards subsequently walk in and stand Pranzini up. He is then escorted out of the prison, with hands bound in front of him. The priest follows closely behind him. The crowd is anything but friendly toward Pranzini as they curse and throw things at him. This amuses him. They would all be joining him somewhere down the road.

While this is happening, Thérèse enters a small chapel some distance away and kneels before a crucifix. Staring straight ahead, she begins to pray.

"Lord, I am sure you will pardon your unfortunate child, Pranzini."

The crowd yells.

"YOU'LL BURN IN HELL, YOU CHILDKILLING DOG!!!"

Thérèse continues.

"I'll believe this even if he shows no sign of repentance."

Someone from the crowd whips Pranzini in the face with a pearl necklace.

"HOW DO YOU LIKE THE NECKLACE YOU SPINELESS COWARD!? ISN'T THAT WHAT YOU MURDERED THOSE WOMEN FOR!?"

Pranzini and his escorts walk up the steps to the guillotine.

Thérèse looks up at the crucifix.

"I will only ask you for a sign, Lord, for my own consolation, if it pleases you."

Pranzini suddenly stops before reaching the guillotine. He can't explain why, nor does he have time to, but he faces the priest behind him, unable to look directly at him. Tears begin to form in his eyes.

"Bring me the cross!"

The priest holds his Crucifix up to Pranzini. Pranzini grabs it out of his hands and kisses the wounds of Christ, slowly and tenderly, and gives the Crucifix back to the priest. The priest makes the Sign of the Cross over Pranzini.

"My son...may God bless you."

Pranzini looks off into the distance with tears freely flowing down his face, still not sure why, but feeling a freedom unlike anything he has ever experienced in all his days of "adventuring."

"He already has."

Pranzini is positioned in the guillotine.

Thérèse finishes her prayer.

"Amen."

Chapter 3

Thérèse...

Well, I've done everything I can. Celine has assured me that she had mass said for Pranzini's conversion and I have prayed for him the best I know how. I know God must have saved him, but now I want to see if He'll give me a sign. I'm standing close to the street outside my house, waiting for the newspaper. It is finally dropped in front of me. I quickly pick it up and run up my porch steps and back into my house. I unfold the paper, start reading, and there it is... I drop the paper and put my hands over my mouth trying to keep myself from screaming with delight. I hide behind the curtain next to the front door.

Bad decision, but how am I to think straight right now? I soon hear Papa come in through the door. He will have been looking for the paper. I hear him call upstairs, sounding a little frustrated.

"Celine! Did you pick up the paper? It should have come in by now."

"No, Papa. Are you sure?"

If I can just stay quiet...

"...Found it."

Nope, can't hold it anymore. I begin laughing. It's stifled but definitely not quiet. Soon the curtain is pulled from in front of me and I'm caught. Papa looks amused.

"Thérèse? What are you doing behind the curtain?"

It doesn't take him long to put it together as he eyes me and slightly raises the messy newspaper with a hint of disappointment.

"Were you reading the newspaper? You know you're not allowed."

All I can do is smile.

"I'm sorry, Papa. I didn't think I'd be disobeying if I only read about Pranzini." That's the truth…a soul *was* at stake.

Papa looks confused as if he is not sure he heard correctly. I can't blame him.

"Pranzini? The triple-murderer who was just executed yesterday? I cannot think of a worse subject you could be reading about."

I abandon myself with delight and wrap my arms around him. I haven't felt this much joy since last Christmas.

"Papa, he repented! God has given me my first child! I had a mass said for him, prayed for him, and asked for a sign of his repentance and God answered it to the letter! He's in heaven! I know it! Just like the 'Good Thief'!"

Papa was tense when I first embraced him, but after I speak, I feel him relax and return my embrace.

"I am glad to hear that, my queen. Just let me know the next time you want to read the newspaper. You don't have to hide anything from me."

Chapter 4

Pauline...

I've been a Carmelite for...how long now? It doesn't feel long, but time seems to pass unnoticed in these walls. Papa and my two younger sisters have come to visit me and my older sister Marie, who, ironically, didn't enter Carmel until after I did. We've had a nice visit in spite of these bars that separate us...and the fact that Thérèse hasn't said a word. She seems quite subdued.

After I tell them good-bye, they start approaching the exit, but Thérèse does not follow, and she finally speaks up.

"Papa? Can I have some time alone with Pauline and Marie?"

Pauline...that name sounds more and more foreign to me since everyone else calls me Agnes, the name I took when I entered Carmel. It is easier for Marie since she kept her name and simply added something to it.

Papa knows there is a mother-daughter-like relationship between Thérèse and myself. Since Mama died, I know it has been something he has appreciated. But I also know that since my entrance, it must have been like losing a second mother for her.

Papa smiles at Thérèse.

"Of course. Celine and I will wait outside."

Celine can't help but tease a bit.

"Don't be *too* long."

After the door closes behind them, Thérèse lets her emotions go and begins crying as she falls to her knees, placing her hands around the bars of the grill. I briefly look at Marie and we get up and rush to her. I place my hands over hers.

"Don't cry, Thérèse. Tell me what's on your mind."

She can barely choke out the words. It seems she has had a lot pent up inside of her and now it's all coming out at once.

"Not my mind, but my heart: an unquenchable thirst to bring souls to God…"

"Why does it make you cry?" I thought she had finally outgrown her hypersensitivity.

"It's driving me *here*. It wants me here *now*! Jesus is calling me here, *now*, to our desert!"

She continues crying and leans her head against the bars.

Somehow I am not surprised. I think back to the miraculous cure Thérèse received for her mysterious illness from Our Lady of Victories, when all seemed lost. Perhaps it was leading up to this? I move my face inches from hers and I almost shout.

"Then do not be afraid! Follow Him!"

Thérèse stops crying and looks up at me, her face still covered in tears and a look of wonder in her eyes.

Marie, or Sister Marie of the Sacred Heart, if you like, sounds just a little outraged by my response.

"Thérèse! You are not even fifteen! Mama has died, the two of us are already here, and Leonie is in the Visitation at Caen; not to mention our other brothers and sisters who have already died at such young ages. You are Papa's youngest! If you leave him so soon, it will destroy him!"

I know there is no use getting into an argument, so I look at Thérèse with a subtle hint of humor, hoping that she will catch it.

"Maybe, Marie's right, Thérèse. Just forget it. Think about Papa."

I can tell she understands, as she smiles with gratitude, and kisses my hand before running off.

Chapter 5

Celine...

What happened in there with Pauline? Thérèse has barely been speaking to anyone. Since we visited our sisters, she has looked more and more weighed down with each passing day. It's time to pry. Maybe she's trying to figure out how to convert another serial killer or something. I go to our room and find her sitting on her bed, lost in thought. She looks really tired and barely notices me when I come in.

"Thérèse? Is everything alright? You've seemed distant lately, withdrawn."

Thérèse slowly faces toward me, but doesn't look at me. It's almost like she's just waking up.

"Have I? I'm sorry."

I sit down close beside her on the bed.

"What's going on with you?"

"I don't want to make you sad."

What is this? Last time she didn't want to make me laugh. I put an arm around her.

"And I don't want you to endure whatever you're going through by yourself."

Thérèse sorrowfully looks into my eyes.

"Celine, I have to leave. Jesus is calling me to Carmel, now, and I don't know how to tell Papa, and I didn't know how to tell you. I know we have the same destiny, to make Jesus our spouse, and you have more of a right to enter before me, since you're older. But I have to go, *now*."

I look away from Thérèse. I knew she was called to this, and I even guessed it might be sooner rather later, but that doesn't stop it from stinging nonetheless. Yet as I look down, trying to hold back tears, somehow I know this is from God, and that my sister will need all the support she can get. I smile and I look back at Thérèse.

"You're right. Our destinies are the same. Right now, however, mine involves seeing you off. I'll do whatever I can to help. Tell Papa. He loves you more than you know. He will see that this is God's will for you, as I do, and you will get his blessing, as you have mine."

Thérèse wraps her arms around me and I do likewise.

Chapter 6

Thérèse…

I see Papa sitting on a well outside, with his hands folded, appearing to be in deep thought, nature's beauty radiant behind him. As I approach him, I can feel my chest getting tighter and tighter. I don't know how this is going to work. Marie, Pauline, and Leonie, that was one thing---or three---but now me, his "queen"? All I can do as I draw closer to him is pray and try not to cry. That has always been a pretty frustrating habit. Always crying at the drop of a hat. Even crying about crying… Was this not actually worth crying over, though?

As I slowly sit down beside my father, my "king", my resistance to tears quickly fails. Papa immediately notices and gently guides my head to his chest.

"What's wrong my little queen? Tell me."

The words come out choked and abrupt.

"Papa, I must enter Carmel now."

He stands up with my head still pressed to his chest, and begins walking with me. I guess he's taking his time, processing. He then responds gently.

"You're very young to be making such a serious decision."

My emotions pour out. I've kept this from him for too long.

"The decision is not mine, but my belovéd Jesus's. He is calling me there now, Papa. I know it! It started with a thirst that arose in me to win souls for Him, which drove me to pray for Pranzini. Now I know He calls me to win so many more at Carmel. He wants me there to Himself…AND EVERY DAY I AM UNABLE TO ANSWER THIS CALL IS PURE AGONY! PLEASE PAPA! HELP ME!"

Papa stops walking. My words must be like a knife to his heart. He holds me tighter. After what feels like an eternity, I feel his breath on top of my head.

"I will, my child. I promise you."

I feel his cheek rest on top of my head, and after a few moments, he lets me go.

I can hardly believe what I just heard nor the confidence and reassurance in my father's dark eyes. Is this real?

He takes me by the hand, and we begin walking again, looking off into the horizon. As we walk, he suddenly smiles and looks at me again.

"God is giving me quite an honor, taking my children away from me. Four He has taken to be with Him in Heaven, two to Carmel, one to the Visitation…and now He comes for my little queen." He pauses. "So much the better…"

Chapter 7

It's not long, but it feels like forever, waiting to go back to Carmel and share my joy. When I arrive, I feel *delirious* with joy and I practically fall into the cloister bars before Pauline.

"Pauline! It's happening! Papa said, 'Yes!'"

Pauline is silent as she looks at me with a sense of...pity?

"What is it?"

"Our superior, Father Delatroëtte, is denying your entrance until you are twenty-one."

I can only sigh. I should have known it wouldn't be that easy.

***

I return home and give Papa the news. He doesn't seem discouraged at all. Maybe he's relieved? But he surprises me.

"Don't worry about it. We'll go see the bishop. The Carmel Superior may have refused, but the bishop has authority over him. If the bishop refuses, well...we are already set for a pilgrimage to Rome; we'll take it to the Pope!"

***

It is pouring down rain when we arrive at the bishop's residence in Bayeux. I have my hair done up for a change and I decided maybe black would be a better dress color for this occasion. Papa knocks on the big double doors, which open to reveal a priest who I suppose is an aide to the bishop. This guy looks kind of creepy, but he smiles warmly and invites us in.

"How may I help you today?"

Papa removes his goofy looking top-hat, while holding my hand.

"Father Révérony, thank you for having us. I am Louis Martin and this is my daughter Thérèse. We are here to see Bishop Hugonin. My daughter has a vocation to religious life at the Carmel of Lisieux that demands her immediate entrance. The Carmel Superior has refused to allow this, so we are hoping that the bishop will be able to help."

Well said Papa. Father Révérony looks like he's not sure if he heard right.

"This daughter with you now?" He turns to me with a smile. "…And how old are you, my dear?"

This is quickly beginning to feel awkward.

"I turn fifteen in three months…"

Father Révérony lets out a slight hint of laughter. *Yeah, ha, ha, Father.* I guess this will go nowhere. He maintains a sense of politeness.

"I am going to introduce you to the bishop; will you kindly follow me?"

As we walk down an ornate hall, lined with portraits of the previous bishops of Bayeux, I repeatedly tell myself "You will not cry! You will not cry! You will not cry!" But I can already feel tears starting to bubble in my eyes.

Father Révérony stops, putting his hand on the handle of the door to the bishop's office while looking back at us, and notices my tears. *Great.* He tries to address me in a comforting and humorous tone.

"Oohh, I see diamonds. You can't let the bishop see them." He gently wipes my face with his handkerchief. "That's better." *We'll see.*

He opens the door to reveal a large office with a balcony in the background where the bishop is standing with two other priests, their backs turned to us. We begin approaching his desk. As we do, Papa whispers to me.

"What's wrong?"

I whisper shrilly.

"I feel like a tiny *ant* about to be stepped on! What will I say to the bishop?"

Papa tries to reassure me.

"Calm down. God will decide what happens here."

We stop close to two large chairs in front of the bishop's desk as Father Révérony proceeds onto the balcony behind the desk. He and the bishop exchange words for a few moments as I begin to feel smaller and smaller. The bishop makes a motion dismissing the two priests and they follow Father Révérony past me and Papa, politely acknowledging us on their way, and leave the office, closing the door behind them. *Here we go.*

The bishop walks in, looking at us from behind his desk, smiling.

"Ah...Monsieur Martin and his young daughter, Thérèse...welcome." He gestures with his hand. "Please...have a seat."

We sit, while the bishop remains standing behind his desk. This chair I'm sitting in is huge. It's almost like it's trying to eat me. The bishop casually looks left and right at us.

"And what can I do for you today?"

Papa is comfortably slouched to the side in his chair. Time for him to shine.

"Thank you, Bishop, for seeing us today." He motions to me and a cold rush surges through my body. "Thérèse, why don't you tell the bishop why we are here?"

I cannot believe he just said that. I took for granted that Papa would do all of the talking. No going back now. I clear my throat and speak as formally as a fifteen-year-old-in-three-months can muster.

"Excellency...I desire to enter the Carmel of Lisieux...I have desired this for a long time and have come to realize that the Lord is calling me there, now, in spite of how young I am. The Lisieux Carmel Superior refuses to allow it, but has conceded that he would have nothing to say against your permission should you grant it." That came out better than I expected.

The bishop's smiling expression is unchanged as he maintains an unreadable tone.

"You've desire this for a long time, you say?"

Stay calm. "Yes, Bishop...a *very* long time."

"Come now, you cannot say it has been *fifteen years* since you began to feel this call."

Breathe! "That's... true...but there aren't too many years to subtract because I have wanted to be a religious since the dawn of my reason, and

I wanted Carmel as soon as I knew about it…I find all the aspirations of my soul are fulfilled in this Order."

The bishop gently laughs in his throat and bows his head slightly, then, raising his head back up, tilts his gaze toward Papa.

"Do not worry, Monsieur Martin, *I am on your side.* We will have your daughter remain with you for at least a few more years. Now if you would excuse me…"

Papa quickly sits up.

"Hold on. I apologize. I did not mean to give the wrong impression. I agree with my daughter that God is calling her immediately into Carmel and I fully stand behind her in her decision." *About time, Papa…*

The bishop's expression becomes more serious and betrays some surprise.

"Monsieur Martin…men like you are a true gift to the Church; so willing to give all that is precious to you to God without hesitation or counting the cost."

Papa relaxes. "Thank you, Bishop."

I think maybe we're getting somewhere, but the bishop isn't finished.

"However, before I can grant such a radical request, I must consult with the Superior of Carmel myself."

I can't take it. *Not again…*

"I just told you of his refusal!"

"Yes…yes you did."

Futile. I rest my face in my hand. Time for some "diamonds."

I hear the bishop move around his desk to me. He tenderly touches my cheek and tries to encourage me. Not that it will do much good.

"My child…all is not lost."

I feel him actually embrace me and I react by hiding my eyes in his shoulder as he continues to try to comfort me.

"I understand you are going to Rome on pilgrimage. This will strengthen your vocation all the more and is cause for rejoicing, not sadness. Next week, before I go to Lisieux, I will discuss you with the pastor of St. James and you will receive my answer while you are in Italy."

***

It is still pouring rain outside of the bishop's residence. I am walking with no regard for the rain, which is soaking me. In spite of the coldness of the rain, my cheeks still feel hot from embarrassment.

Papa and Father Révérony are casually following me while carrying umbrellas. I can hear Papa asking questions to the priest.

"So how should one dress for a pilgrimage to Rome? Am I good as I am?"

I don't look back, but I can guess that Papa made some sort of clown-like pose. Father Révérony responds with a laugh. Papa continues.

"You know, Thérèse put up her hair for the bishop to make herself look older?"

Father Révérony laughs all the more. "We noticed!"

At this, I tense up with anger.

Well, at least they're having fun.

I undo my hair, letting it down, and begin walking faster.

Chapter 8

Celine…

Papa, Thérèse, and I get off of a train in a Roman station. Papa quickly gives instructions.

"You two wait right here, while I grab our luggage."

While Papa is gone I try to encourage Thérèse. I know she still feels a lack of confidence after what happened with the bishop.

"We're finally in Rome, Thérèse. Soon we'll get to meet the Pope and all that will be left after that is to pray."

"That thought both scares me and gives me peace."

"No doubt."

A commotion arises in the train station. It seems school has let out and a bunch of students, most of whom seem older than me, start passing through. *What is taking Papa so long?*

"I'll see what's keeping Papa," I tell Thérèse as I walk off. I hear her behind me pleading.

"Celine!"

I admit it was stupid to leave her alone, but I don't think too well in noisy crowds. I go for some distance looking for Papa and then I hear a shriek.

"CELINE!"

I turn around and see one of the students has Thérèse in his grip and is pulling her toward two of his friends who are motioning for him to hurry towards them. Yeah, that *was* stupid. I shout her name as I try to push my way through the increasingly claustrophobic crowd. I see her ahead struggling with no success; she's barely half the boy's size. I don't know if

I'm going to make it over before they disappear with her, but even if I do, then what? *Where is Papa?*

The boy is laughing while pulling Thérèse along, as she futilely tries to squirm out of his grip. They are getting further away from me, but then Thérèse stops struggling and looks up at the boy. The boy is looking toward his friends, but then briefly glances down at her and stops in his tracks. A look of utter terror comes over his face. He slowly releases his grip, and Thérèse, after looking at him a moment longer, turns around and begins making her way toward me. We finally meet and I put a hand on Thérèse's shoulder and look back at the boy who is still frozen as he was, gazing at Thérèse. I'd love to know what it is he sees, but there is no way I am going to ask. All that matters is that Thérèse is safe. *Oh, there's Papa…*

***

Thérèse…

St. Peter's Basilica; made it in one piece…barely. The sooner I'm in Carmel, the better. It is beautiful getting to see Pope Leo XIII blessing Papa. If he knew Papa, I wonder if he'd want the favor returned. After Papa gets up, Celine goes ahead of me and receives his blessing. My cause already seems lost here. We were instructed as we entered not to speak to the pope. Something about him being ill… That's going to make two of us if I'm outside of Carmel much longer. The pope finishes with Celine and, as she stands up, she looks back at me with a smile. It gives me the confidence I need. I didn't come all this way and almost get kidnapped for nothing…

I take a breath and kneel down, bowing my head. I feel the pope's hand on top of my head. It's quite warm and his voice is soothing as he blesses me. I feel his hand lift up and then come back down. *It's now or never…*

I gently take his hand into my hands and lower them to rest in his lap, not realizing that my eyes had already filled with tears as he blessed me. My words come out a bit choked.

"Most Holy Father, I have a great favor to ask you."

He smiles warmly at me and lowers his head almost touching mine. His black eyes are so piercing, I have to close mine as I speak.

"Holy Father, in honor of your Jubilee, permit me to enter Carmel at the age of fifteen."

I look back into his eyes which seem to pierce my soul. He answers me, his voice very gentle.

"I'm sorry, I did not understand."

He didn't hear me? I repeat it louder, feeling the stares of others around us.

"I'm fifteen and I want to enter Carmel. Please help me."

He smiles.

"Oh…well I can presume you already have superiors considering this matter. Do what they tell you."

"But if you permit it, *everyone* will agree."

The pope places his other warm hand on my cheek. Gentle and encouraging.

"My child…*go*…you will enter if it is God's will."

The pope moves his hand away. I can only continue to gaze at him. I feel a tap on my shoulder, one of those oddly dressed guards. I don't budge. I then feel a set of hands wrap underneath both of my arms as I am lifted to my feet. I try to protest, but the pope gently places his fingers on my lips and then makes the Sign of the Cross on my forehead. The guards continue to hold my arms as I am taken away.

Chapter 9

Pauline...

Poor Thérèse...all she's gone through and here we are, still separated by these bars. There's a look of resignation on her face, like she's giving up. I can't blame her. We've been sitting in silence for a while. Finally she speaks.

"I don't know what else to do, Pauline. It's been two months since I got back from Rome and I haven't heard anything, even after writing the bishop to remind him."

"Don't give up hope, Thérèse. I almost did. I found myself in prayer actually reproaching God for allowing so many obstacles to hinder you. You know what happened? *He* reproached me! He said 'Am I not the Master of hearts? Which is better, to listen to My voice or that of the blind and senseless world?... I will be stronger than all of you. I *want* this child. She is a lily-bud opened before the dawn. She is a fruit ripened before the autumn. From on high, I have desired this lily, the beauty of this fruit... My divine hand is ready to pluck my treasure...Who will dare say to me: Lord it is too soon, if *I* find that it is time?' One way or another, Thérèse, you'll find your way in here. Even if it's not right now."

She is about to respond but is interrupted by the door opening and closing behind me.

I look up and see the Prioress, Mother Marie de Gonzague, standing over us, looking down at Thérèse through the bars.

"Mother...?" Before I can say another word she begins speaking.

"I thought you would still be here, little Thérèse, so I wanted to let you know in person. I received notice from our superior, not long after your return from Rome, that your entrance...has been approved. I decided to delay informing you, however, because your entrance is not to be until after the completion of Lent."

I already know how Thérèse is going to respond, but before I can stop her, she yells.

"That's three months!"

Mother Prioress scolds her.

"Gracious, child! That is a far shorter wait than what I would recommend! Be grateful for what you are being given."

I could have been invisible this whole time, but then the Prioress turns her attention to me.

"Sister Agnes, do not be too much longer. There is work to be done."

Thérèse and I are alone again and I smile at her. *Finally.*

"Well there you have it."

I notice the look of dissatisfaction on Thérèse's face. I can't help but laugh.

"Thérèse, these next three months will be a good opportunity for you to really prepare yourself for Carmel. Be patient, and use them to build charity in your heart and overcome your stubbornness."

"How should I go about that?"

"Well, we already know how prayerful you are, but some acts of penance might be another good step. Look…you will be among us before you know it. Give these next three months to God the best you know how. After all, when you come in here, you'll be giving Him your entire life."

***

Thérèse…

Three months. I have to wait three more months. I know that's not much, but it still feels like eternity. I guess I might be getting a taste of what Purgatory is like.

We're all eating dinner together. Well, Celine and I are, Papa is just staring at me with a smile.

"It won't be long, now, my queen."

Celine chimes in while smiling at Papa.

"And don't worry. Papa won't be alone."

"By the way, I've noticed you've been sitting kind of odd lately."

It's almost becoming automatic for me.

"Pauline suggested that I take on some penances to help me prepare for my entrance. I'm too weak for penances, so I'm just trying to at least have some little mortifications, like not imposing my will on others, holding back sharp replies, and…not leaning my back against a support when seated."

Papa suddenly looks past me, his eyes widening in fear, and then he stands up abruptly, causing me to bolt back in my chair. Celine speaks first.

"Papa! What is it?"

He stares for a moment longer and then snaps out of it, shaking his head slightly.

"It's nothing. Eyes must have been playing tricks on me. I seem to have a bit of a headache. I'm going to lie down for a little while."

He walks around the table and out of the dining room, our gaze following him. I look at Celine.

"What was that?"

Celine looks as confused as I am.

"I don't know…maybe something he ate?"

But he didn't eat anything…

Part II

Beyond The Bars

Chapter 10

Thérèse...

I stand with what's left of my family. Behind me is the desert I've dreamed of since I was five years old. Where I am going, they cannot follow. Even if Celine were to enter, I know that she could not any longer be Celine any more than my two other sisters could be who they were outside these walls. I embrace her and my "King" for the last time. Then I turn around and approach the entrance. The double doors open before me to a host of Carmelites making a path for me. As I walk through them, it is as though I am in a dream. The doors close behind me, and I am in another world.

Before I know it, I am on my knees in the convent chapel, no longer wearing my own clothes, but the clothes of a Carmelite. Mother Marie de Gonzague, my new mother, stands beside Bishop Hugonin who reads out loud from a huge book. I don't hear what he says. All I can hear is my heart pounding. All the Carmelites of the convent surround us. Pauline---no---*Sister Agnes* stands before me with the white veil and mantle folded over her arms that will seal my new identity. Sister Marie of the Sacred Heart cuts my hair. When she finishes, Sister Agnes unfolds the white garments, giving the mantle to Sister Marie of the Sacred Heart, who places it around my shoulders. Sister Agnes kneels down beside me, kisses me on the cheek, and places the white veil on my head. I feel my heart rate slow. Marie-Françoise-Thérèse Martin is dead. My name is Sister Thérèse of the Child Jesus and the Holy Face.

***

After the ceremony, I am with Mother Marie de Gonzague walking briskly down a corridor. Time to learn about my new home. We walk into a dining area, which in here is called a "refectory." Don't ask me why. Mother Prioress exhorts me not to complain if the meals here seem rather simple. So much the better. I've never particularly cared for the ceremony and hysteria that seems to surround meals.

We walk back into the Carmelite chapel and Mother continues orienting me.

"You've seen this area, but I show it to you again because you will be cleaning this room regularly in addition to tending laundry. And please don't forget to clean the corners of the windows."

In one of those windows there is a spider web, occupied by a large spider. I really hate spiders. *Good.*

We step outside into the garden. There is a large Crucifix mounted on a post in the center. It is a beautiful site to me. Mother continues explaining.

"This is our garden. We come out here, not only to grow food but also to engage in some recreations or just to enjoy the outdoors."

I see my two sisters sitting on a bench together some distance away. The Prioress sees them too.

"Excuse me for a moment."

She begins walking over toward them. I guess we need to learn to be Sisters rather than sisters. It is something of a wonder that my *age* was the main issue that stalled my entrance and not the fact that I already have two blood sisters in here.

I step back to get a better look at this crucifix and as I do, I feel someone bump into me from behind. A middle-aged nun practically walks through me before turning around to face me in anger.

"Watch it!"

Without hesitation, I kneel down and kiss the ground. I then stand back up and smile at her. She just shakes her head and keeps walking while muttering something about me being Mother's new pet. I place my hand on the base of the Crucifix.

Soon after, the Prioress and I enter a small wooden cell with a bed and a desk. A Crucifix is also on the wall. Mother turns to me.

"And finally…this is your cell. Any questions? Do you think you'll actually be able to handle it here at your age?"

It makes me smile.

"I am here forever."

Mother Marie de Gonzague eyes me.

"Hmph…very well then," and leaves without further comment.

I am here forever.

Chapter 11

Marie...

So my youngest sister is among us. It was no surprise that Pauline entered, even if it was before me, but I never would have guessed: Thérèse at *fifteen*! How will this work? At least Mother Prioress has given me instructions to watch after her.

We are gathering for lunch in the refectory. I see Thérèse eating some soup, sitting with her back away from the rest---that can't be comfortable. I sit beside her, smiling. She smiles back, but then just keeps eating without a word. Is she angry?

"It's wonderful that you made it in here with us, Thérèse. I hope you are not angry with me for not having been supportive."

"Not even a little."

She keeps eating. I decide to change the subject.

"Have you gotten to meet everyone?"

She lightly sets down her spoon.

"Not yet."

"Well, since everyone is here, let me point some of them out."

I direct her attention over to Mother Prioress.

"You of course already know our Prioress, Mother Marie de Gonzague. She has been Prioress here for 27 years. It's only a matter of time before someone else is elected."

I point to another older nun with a more pleasant bearing than our Prioress.

"Over there is Sister Marie of the Angels. She is the Novice Mistress, so you will be in her charge."

I should also make her aware of that nun she ran into, or rather that nun that ran into her, in the garden.

"That 'nice' lady you met during your tour is Sister St. Vincent de Paul. Try not to let her get to you."

Lastly I point out our senior. "Oh, also there is Sister St. Pierre, the oldest in our community. I don't know why she continues to demand to be brought to the refectory and to choir. We could just as easily serve her in her cell. It's such a pain..."

Oh, and speaking of being preceded by my younger sister.

"You know, I heard rumors that suggest that Pauline might become our next prioress!? So we may get to call her "Mother" Agnes. It has a good ring to it."

"You still call her Pauline?"

"Yes, *Thérèse*. And I hope you still call me Marie. Before I forget, I've been assigned as your 'angel.' I am to help you get fully oriented with all the details of life here---prayer and otherwise."

"Thank you...*Sister Marie of the Sacred Heart*, but listen: I've left Les Buissonnets behind. It hurts to say this, but I think it's important: try to let me manage on my own as much as possible."

I feel a bit at a loss. What's happened to my baby sister? This is good, though; she's not angry, or even trying to be rude, she's just determined not to look back. I smile and lightly lean my forehead on hers.

"I can already tell that I was wrong about you."

The bell rings and we disperse.

Chapter 12

Celine...

I'm sitting with Papa on our porch in silence. We haven't talked a whole lot since Thérèse's entrance. It's hard to say what I am feeling. I know it was the right thing for Thérèse to enter, but I still feel a sense of loss. I want her to be back here with us, but then we wouldn't really have her. The more she is God's, the more she is ours. As I said, it's difficult to explain what I am feeling... I want to hear Papa say something.

"Are you sad, Papa?"

"...On the contrary: my heart is overflowing with joy for our Thérèse. I'm a happy man."

I nod as I rock in my chair. Papa suddenly jumps in his chair, and I see a look of terror in his eyes. He speaks to me in a low, slightly trembling voice.

"Celine...get in the house."

"What is it Papa?"

He doesn't answer. He just stares in front of us, terrified. I look in the direction of his gaze and I see nothing. I suddenly feel him grab my arm.

"Get in the house now! Do as I say!"

I can feel fear building up in me. *What's happening?* I let him usher me into the house where he sits me against the wall next to the door.

"Wait here!"

He runs off while ducking. I'm feeling hysterics starting to set in as I call after him.

"PAPA!?"

After a few moments of silence, he returns with a revolver in his hand. My threshold for horror is reaching its limit, but I lower my voice.

"Papa?"

Papa flings open the curtain on the other side of the door from me and appears to take cover. He then smashes the window with the butt of the pistol and fires a shot. The bang is so deafening, I can't even hear myself scream. Papa begins shouting out through the window.

"I WON'T LET YOU TAKE US!!!"

I break into hysterical cries.

"PAPA!!! STOP!!!"

He keeps firing while yelling out the window.

"STAY BACK!!!"

I've got to get out of here...get help... I'm still crying and trembling uncontrollably as I get to my feet. Papa doesn't notice me. After he fires another shot and takes cover, in a rush of adrenaline, I fling open the door and run out. I hear him shouting after me.

"CELINE! DON'T GO OUT THERE! IT'S TOO DANGEROUS!!!"

I keep running.

"CELINE!!!"

***

I once heard a saying that hell primarily consists of watching those you love suffer while there is nothing you can do about it. I can't say I agree with that statement, but if it were true, then I could emphatically say that I am living in hell.

I was exhausted when I made it to the hospital and could barely tell them what had happened. I was led to a bed where I curled up into a ball, continuing to weep, and eventually passed out.

I woke up to find a nurse sitting in a chair close by. She told me that Papa was safe---that was the good news. The bad news is what I am now on my way to tell my sisters in Carmel: Papa has gone mad.

I am trying to contain my emotions as the curtain draws back revealing my three sisters behind the bars. It's no good. I fall to my knees, weeping, as I tell them everything that happened with Papa. I see a look of horror erupt on Marie's face who hugs Pauline. Pauline, ever the mature one, simply closes her eyes. I look at Thérèse...*will she blame herself for this?*

To my surprise, she is quiet. She approaches the bars and holds out her hand through them. I slowly get to my feet, go to her, and take her hand. She leans her head against the bars and my head meets hers. She begins speaking to me with a great sense of calm. I don't hear her words as I weep, but something about her voice is making me feel a little less hell.

Chapter 13

Thérèse...

Scripture says that while we are in the world, we are not to be of the world. I have made a vow that one might think could make me not even be *in* the world. Given what happened to my "King," this is obviously not the case. Or at least, while I may not be in the world, the world has managed to break through the cloister bars and find its way in me. Yet how am I responding to my father's humiliation, not to mention my own? Standing right here where I am and folding laundry. I still haven't cried since receiving the news from Celine. In fact, I feel peace. Does this make me crazy? Am I cold? Oh, I still hurt. But there is something to the suffering that God is helping me to see and believe. Something redemptive, random and unjustified though it may appear.

My new novice mistress, Sister Marie of the Angels, folds clothes alongside me. She's a sweet old lady. Very light-hearted. I can feel her gaze on me, however. Then I feel her hand on my shoulder and I stop working.

"Is there anything you'd like to talk about? It must be difficult accepting what happened to your father."

"I'm okay."

"My child, it seems you never have anything to say to your superiors, even with all that's happened with your family."

"Why do you say that, Mother?"

"I think it is because you are very simple. As you draw closer to God, you will become even more simple. Yet perhaps, at some point you will find more ease in expressing yourself without ceasing to be simple."

Without another word we continue working.

41

Chapter 14

Here I am, back on my knees. Time has flown and now I am about to receive the black veil, sealing myself as a Carmelite forever. I should relate some things that led to this point.

First, I don't sit like I had before entering anymore. I had gotten so used to sitting with my back away from a seat rest that I hardly noticed it. This might have continued if not for an incident in the garden during a time of recreation. I was sitting in that manner while knitting. The Prioress happened to be passing by and noticed me.

"Sister Thérèse of the Child Jesus…why are you stooped over like that? That can't be helping your knitting, which takes you long enough as it is."

I smiled. "Prior to entering here, I got in the habit of sitting like this as a mortification."

She smirked a bit, put her hand on my shoulder, and gently pushed me back on the seat rest so that I was sitting upright.

"Mortifying your *self-love* will yield more fruit than merely dwelling on the flesh." She then left without any further word.

I've tried to take these words to heart, especially when I've seen Sister St. Vincent de Paul, but I'll get back to her.

There was another time when we had gathered for quiet prayer in the chapel. After everyone was settled, I enjoyed a brief moment of quiet before becoming aware of a noise behind me. I didn't know what it was at first, but it eventually dawned on me that one of my fellow Sisters right behind me was unconsciously making a light, but repetitive clicking noise with her tongue. I didn't turn around, but I looked around with my eyes to see if anyone else could hear it. Nope. I then just tried to ignore it. The sound continued, however, *on and on and on…* With each click, the sound became more and more exaggerated to me, until it seemed as though someone might as well have just been repeatedly firing off a cannon next to my ear. I could soon feel sweat beginning to trickle down my face.

I'm about to go crazy!

I took a breath, however, and realized the opportunity God was giving me in a seemingly insignificant situation. I decided to focus on the sound rather than trying to ignore it, offering it as a sweet sounding melody to God, and in doing so it became so to me…I think I fell asleep.

I was awoken, however, by the sound of the bell. It was time to go to the refectory. I stood up and noticed old Sister St. Pierre sitting on a bench, shaking an hourglass---her way of signaling that she needs help getting around. Another opportunity. I quickly went over to her to offer assistance.

"Sister? Can I help you get to the refectory?"

"You're too young!"

"Please, Sister, I won't let you down."

The old nun didn't look convinced, but nodded her head. Good enough.

I helped her to her feet and she cried out.

"Easy! I'm dying you know!"

I laughed. "Sister, you're not dying…"

We slowly made our way to the refectory and I got her seated in spite of her lamenting. I then rolled up her sleeves and almost walked away, but I noticed she was struggling with the bread. I squatted down and gestured for her to give me the knife, and I cut the bread into small pieces, and smiled at her. A sense of surprised delight erupted on her face and she put her hand on my cheek.

"Thank you, child. No one has ever treated me this *kindly* before. I always feel like such a burden." I kissed her hand and went to my place.

Little things.

Chapter 15

Not long after this, Sister Agnes came down with a bad nosebleed, and this would prove to be the herald of the most challenging and sad, while at the same time, blessed occasion of my novitiate: an influenza epidemic that brought the Carmel to its knees. Somehow, I did not catch it, which meant that I had to be on my feet basically all of the time, trying to attend to the needs of dozens of my fellow Sisters who had. One particular night would see me assist Sister St. Pierre again in a particularly unique way.

I had prepared a tray of food and was bringing it to her. As soon as I entered her cell, I could sense that something was different. She was laying on her side faced away from me. I put the tray on her desk and sat down at her bedside. Placing my hand on her shoulder, my suspicion was confirmed when I gently turned her over to face me. While I was not surprised, I still felt a shudder as I closed her eyes and prayed for her. I then got up and walked to our storage room to get a blessed candle and wreath to set as a memorial for her. There was nothing more I could do for her, and I could hear the moans and vomiting of my other Sisters pouring into Sister St. Pierre's cell as I stood over her and brushed away some tears from my face.

I then picked up the tray and proceeded into the neighboring cell which happens to belong to Sister Marie of the Sacred Heart. I could already hear her gagging from inside her room, but I did not expect to see Sister Agnes sitting at her bedside holding the bucket for Sister Marie of the Sacred Heart to vomit into. Though her back was to me, I could already tell, from her dark sweaty hair, that my motherly sister was overdoing it by trying to tend to Sister Marie of the Sacred Heart and on top of that she was clearly showing partiality towards her, due to our blood relation, when there were plenty of other sick Sisters that she could have troubled herself with.

It was time to get her out. I set down the tray and placed one hand on Sister Agnes's shoulder and used the other to grip the bucket. After Sister Marie of the Sacred Heart finished, she rolled over on her back with her chest heaving, somehow still looking beautiful in spite of her condition. I took the bucket out of Sister Agnes's hands and set it on the floor as I sat down beside her. I looked at her admonishingly---it was an interesting turn of events given that it was always her that acted as a mother toward me.

"You're in no shape to be playing nurse. Go back to bed."

Of course Sister Agnes was not quick to accept such a change of roles as she strained to speak.

"I'm fine, my nose isn't bleeding anymore."

"You obviously still have a fever…"

"Thérèse, don't worry…"

She was cut off before she could finish by…a nosebleed. I methodically pulled a handkerchief from my pocket and gave it to her as she tried to cover her nose with her hand.

"Yeeaah…go back to bed."

Sister Agnes no longer resisted. She quickly took the handkerchief and left without further word…leaving me to be a mother to my other older sister. I looked at her and motioned my head toward the tray I had brought in.

"That was meant for Sister St. Pierre, but she…won't be needing it now."

My sister coughed, struggling to speak.

"That's the seventh one to be taken by this influenza plague…who'd have thought *you'd* be one of the few left standing?"

I sighed.

"Who'd have thought the sick would be trying to take care of the sick?"

She choked out a weak laugh.

"Pauline…oh, excuse me…I mean Sister Agnes…will go a long way here."

"If she lives long enough."

She eyed me questioningly.

"All of this sickness and death that you're having to tend to, and you don't seem the least bit afraid."

"Simple, I know God is watching over us...even now."

"How?"

I thought of Sister St. Pierre...

"I can't even begin to tell you the expressions of peace I have seen on the Sisters' faces whose eyes I've had to close. Whether we live or we die we are in God's hands."

Sister Marie of the Sacred Heart smiled at me, speaking as the nausea began to grip her again.

"I think you'll go a long way too..."

I responded as I lifted the bucket right on time while she began to vomit.

"Time will tell."

Chapter 16

Now what of my want-to-be nemesis? A good place to start is a night, not long after the Community's influenza started to subside, when I was in the chapel helping Sister Marie of the Angels clean the place up. When we had finished she gave me the keys to the Communion grating.

"Return these to Mother Prioress's room, but be sure to do it quietly. She is having to rest, since she is suffering again from her bronchial attacks."

Poor Mother, for all the strength and sternness she demonstrates in her interactions with us, her health always tends to show how human she is. I quietly approached Mother Marie de Gonzague's partially closed cell. As I did, Sister St. Vincent de Paul approached me. Almost out of reflex, I smiled at her. It took some time, but I was becoming as accustomed to smiling at her as I had to sitting the way I used to with by back away from a seat rest.

She noticed the keys in my hands.

"Give those to me! You're clumsy and you'll wake Mother if you go in there."

I kept my smile. "Don't worry, I'll be careful. Sister Marie of the Angels told me to return the keys and I need to obey."

We had been whispering, but Sister St. Vincent de Paul took it up a notch.

"Give them to me!"

She snatched the keys from my hands, causing them to make a loud jingle.

We then heard Mother's weakened voice from inside her cell.

"Who's there? Could you please keep it down?"

My smile faded. Sister St. Vincent de Paul glared at me before storming into the Prioress's cell. I felt a sense of wavering as I heard her speak angrily from inside the cell.

"I am so sorry, Mother! Sister Thérèse of the Child Jesus, for whatever reason, caused the commotion that disturbed you. She is too young and clumsy for our community; I don't know what can be done about her…"

She went on and I began to feel like I might walk in and try to defend myself. I was possessed by a better idea, however, as I walked away with a smile.

As I approached my cell, I came across Sister Marie of the Sacred Heart, who was back on her feet---and no, I will not just call her "Marie."

"What are you smiling about?"

"I was just taking the keys of the Communion grating back to Mother Prioress's cell, and another Sister tried to take them from me, but I resisted, since it was *my* task. Ultimately she had her way, and it caused a commotion that disturbed our sick Mother, for which I was blamed."

"And this makes you happy?"

I almost felt like I did when telling Papa about what happened with Pranzini.

"Yes! Because I did not try to justify myself, though I was very tempted! I just walked away, and here I am, at peace."

"Who was the Sister that you had this run-in with?"

"That's not important."

"It was Sister St. Vincent de Paul wasn't it?" My eldest sister has always been quick, but I kept quiet.

"I thought so. Try to stay away from her. She is a really troublesome presence for the whole community and she seems to have had it out for you since your entrance."

I didn't hesitate. "All the more reason for me to be kind to her!"

She looked surprised by this response so I continued.

"It's true that everything about her is…disagreeable to me. Her words, actions, character…but she is a holy religious who must be pleasing to God. In my encounters with her, I have, and I continue to pray for her and offer to God all of her merits. I think this pleases Him, because artists like to be told of the beauty of their work, and God is the artist of souls! Most of all, I just try to treat her with love."

Sister Marie of the Sacred Heart looked like she agreed with me, but she couldn't help wanting to keep on trying to be my "big sister."

"I still think you should keep your distance, if anything just so she won't be able to get you in trouble again."

I just shrugged my shoulders. That kind of self-preservation isn't needed here.

***

The next day we were back in the garden for recreation. I saw Sister St. Vincent de Paul knitting by herself and so I went and sat by her, with a pencil in one hand and paper in my other hand. I had been wanting to try to write some poetry. Sister St. Vincent de Paul, however, was caught off guard and dropped her knitting. I picked it up and handed it to her while smiling. Nothing seemed to annoy her more than when I smiled at her, but I couldn't help it.

She spoke with a suspicious tone. "What is it with you?"

"What do you mean, Sister?"

"Every time I see you, you give me this ridiculous smile."

I was a little at loss on how to explain. "I'm just happy to see you..."

"Why?"

"Why not?"

She must have thought I was playing her for a fool. "You're trouble."

I smiled and looked directly in her eyes and spoke with a tone of both mischief and gravity. "Oh, I'm *faaar* more imperfect than you know. Will you pray for me?"

Sister St. Vincent de Paul's eyes widened briefly, as she studied me with a sense of confusion.

She stuttered. "I'll...try."

We haven't had any trouble since.

Chapter 17

It was in this very chapel that I kneel in now, that a test began that I did not expect. I was in prayer when I suddenly got hit with a heavy sense of doubt about my vocation.

I'm wrong! This is all wrong!

Sister Agnes kneeled beside me as that thought echoed in my head.

"Are you ready for the big day tomorrow, to wear one of these?" gesturing to her black veil.

I didn't answer. She tried to dig.

"Are you okay?"

I could only whisper.

"I don't think so…"

***

I found Sister Marie of the Angels walking down the hall. It felt better to get this over with sooner rather than later. I might have startled her a little as I ran up behind her.

"Mother, I must speak with you!"

She seemed to sum me up immediately.

"Feeling nervous about tomorrow, I see."

"Worse than that! I don't have a vocation! I fear I have been misleading you and myself this whole time! I love Carmel, but it seems I am only doing my will and not God's will!"

After I finished speaking, I felt confused. Somehow the weight of the thoughts were lightened by turning them into spoken words. Suddenly they held no meaning, no gravity.

My novice mistress just smiled.

"Hmmm...I smell sulfur. Listen, it's quite natural to suffer anxiety right before entering one's vocation, whether it's what *we* do, or marriage, or the priesthood. I heard of a man who was about to become a priest, and on the day of his ordination, he would not leave the sacristy. His priest mentor spoke with him, asking what was wrong. The poor man said 'I can't do this! I'm not worthy!' His mentor responded, 'Of course you're not worthy! Now get out there, it's time!' And he grabbed him by his shoulder and pushed him out."

She gently shoved me after saying this. I started walking. The lie of my doubt had been exposed, but I still needed to do one more thing.

"I'm going to talk to Mother Prioress."

"Why? You know you're called."

"This will ensure it!"

***

I found Mother Marie de Gonzague seated on a bench in the garden, apparently resting. She reminded me of Papa when I came to him to pour my heart out. Yet that was to get in here. This would seem to be the opposite, but was really the fulfillment, to get me to stay.

She began to stand before noticing me walking up. I didn't feel like I could speak until she prompted me.

"Yes?"

I mechanically repeated what I had told my Novice Mistress.

"Mother, I don't have a vocation. I fear I have been misleading you and myself this whole time. I love Carmel, but it seems I am only doing my will and not God's will. I'm not sure I should take the veil tomorrow."

Mother Marie de Gonzague looked at me and we had a moment of very awkward silence. She then did something that I don't know if I'll ever see her do again: erupt with laughter that went on and on for I don't know how long. Then as suddenly as she started, she stopped. Her expression settled back to her usual reserved mannerism, and she walked off without saying another word.

I realize now, as I gaze at my Prioress, who is about to have me sealed with the black veil, that that was her way of telling me to not be afraid, and her laughter scared all the remaining demons away that were causing me to doubt. I lay down prostrate before her surrounded by my Sisters, my hands extended horizontally in imitation of the Cross. I get back up onto my knees. I feel the veil weigh down on my head.

Chapter 18

Thérèse, Pauline, and Marie are standing behind the bars in the visiting parlor with Celine on the other side standing behind Louis who is seated in a wheelchair. There is a blank stare in his eyes and his hair has grayed a bit from his debilitating illness which, unbeknownst to him or his family, had resulted from a series of strokes.

Marie sadly calls out to him.

"Papa? Can you hear me?"

Celine tries to explain.

"The doctor says he probably doesn't have much time left. Papa has moments of clarity every now and then, but most of the time…he's like this," looking down at him sadly.

Pauline tries to be positive and gestures toward Thérèse.

"Papa? You can see Thérèse can't you…what she's wearing? She's one of us now. I know you're proud of her, even if you…can't express it." Pauline's voice chokes a bit as she finishes speaking.

A bell rings. Celine knows it is time to go and gives a timid wave to her sisters. As she begins to turn the wheelchair around, Louis subtly makes eye contact with Thérèse, and gives the slightest hint of a smile as he is turned away from her. Thérèse's eyes fill with tears as she silently receives her father's gesture.

After being brought back to the infirmary of Bon Sauveur Asylum, Louis lies in bed as a doctor is checking his heartbeat with a stethoscope.

Louis blinks his eyes and looks at the doctor while smiling and speaks to him somewhat horse.

"I know why God allowed me to have this ordeal."

The doctor is pleased to hear his voice for a change and asks him why.

"I've never had any humiliations…and I needed one."

The doctor removes his stethoscope from his ears, resting it around his neck, and stands upright.

"Well this one should certainly count…"

The doctor then notices something off about Louis.

"Monsieur?"

Louis stares off blankly with a warm smile on his face.

***

Marie…

Papa has died. And all we can do is try to go on. The election to determine if we will have the same or a different Prioress is about to conclude. Since there are three of us Martin sisters, we are not allowed to vote. Instead we have been shut up in Thérèse's cell. What nonsense! Mother Marie de Gonzague is just afraid of losing her power. I'm leaning against the wall as Pauline sits on the bed with our apparently traumatized baby sister, trying to reassure her.

"Thérèse, listen to me. Even in our community, there can be a tendency to gossip. Sadly, gossip and mercy do not tend to go together, and I know you've heard some Sisters in our community blaming you for Papa. Don't believe them for a second! You know very well that Papa had experienced some complications even before *any* of us had entered! This is not your f…"

Pauline is interrupted as our "beloved" Prioress suddenly enters the room. She glares at Pauline.

"I believe congratulations are in order, Sister Agnes…"

"What?"

"…or I suppose I should say…*Mother*…Agnes."

I can barely contain my excitement as I bounce off the wall and grab Pauline's shoulder. Mother Marie de Gonzague smirks at our new Prioress with a hint of annoyance, and leaves the room. Thérèse looks at Pauline with a sort of sly romantic smile.

"Looks like now *you're* my visible Jesus."

***

Celine…

I had planned all along to enter Carmel once Papa…no longer needed me, but I wouldn't have guessed I'd be kneeling before Pauline. Marie is cutting my hair. Thérèse waits with the white veil and mantle that I will soon wear. What did it feel like for her when she was in my place?

Good-bye hair…at least long hair. Oh well…

Thérèse unfurls the veil and mantle, handing the mantle to Marie, who places it around my shoulders. Thérèse follows up by placing the veil on my head. I would have thought she'd kiss me on the cheek, but nothing. Whatever…I've been through hell, and now I'm free.

I hear Bishop Hugonin. His voice sounds as sharp as my heart.

"Those who follow the spotless Lamb will go with him, clothed in white. May they always be clothed in innocence as a sign of inner purity."

Finally.

Chapter 19

A new novice...

What's wrong with me? Why can't I fit in? I did well growing up in Paris, but that is being turned against me! I was kicked out of the last convent I tried to join, and things aren't going any better in this one. I can't decide what these so-called religious hate about me more: where I'm from or my youth. Don't they have someone in their ranks who entered that was way younger than me? I wonder how she survived...

I walk by Mother Agnes's open cell, but she's with someone who doesn't look much older than me. Is that the one I heard about who entered at fifteen? What was her name? She looks a bit frightened. I hear Mother Agnes speak to her as I pass by.

"As you no doubt have noticed, we've had quite an influx of novices. Since I have been made Prioress, Mother Marie de Gonzague has taken over as Novice Mistress; however, she has requested..."

Someone interrupts her from down the hall just as I am passing by her cell. Apparently it's on my behalf.

"The little Parisian! No way she'll make it here. You're not in Paris anymore, rich girl!"

I stop in my tracks and clinch my teeth. *What's wrong with these people!?*
"Please leave me alone."

Mother Agnes shouts out her door in the direction of my taunter.
"Enough!"

At least someone's sticking up for me. Not that there's much she can do given how busy she is...not to mention inexperienced having, I understand, been just recently elected for the first time. She goes back inside. I think I will listen in on her conversation. What is it that young nun finds so frightening?

"That was Sister Marie of the Trinity who just walked by. For some reason she is not being received too well by members of the community, and her sensitivity is making things all the more difficult for her."

What sensitivity!? She doesn't know me!

"Anyway, as I was saying, given the situation, it seems it would be good to have someone young *and* wise beyond her years to assist in the duty of Novice Mistress."

The young Sister says what I am thinking.

"...Are you sure, Mother?"

"You'll begin tomorrow."

I'm getting stomped on account of my age and this girl is being made Novice Mistress and put directly over me? All this hatred and they're making children, more or less, into Novice Mistresses? How is *this* Carmel even still running?

The girl suddenly emerges from the Prioress's cell heading in the opposite direction from me, muttering to herself.

"Lord, I am far too little to do this on my own...please do it Yourself through me."

At least she's not arrogant.

***

I love the food here...about as much as I love the company. Or lack thereof...no one will sit by me. Someone almost does, but moves on after recognizing me. I feel tears welling up in my eyes. So this is living in Community? I think I would feel less alone if I were actually alone. I see that *girl* sitting across from me. Why is she looking at me like that?

***

I can't take anymore. I'm not even safe around Jesus. We were in the chapel to pray our night prayers, and even there I got taunted! I was stealthily told that I don't belong here---*in the chapel!* No more. This is my last night here. If I can just control my tears until I get to my cell...

Someone for no apparent reason is standing outside her cell with her door partially open. It's *her*! What is she doing? Going to join in on taunting me even though, *supposedly*, no one is allowed to speak at this hour? These people are unbelievable...

She looks at me and I look at her, trying to control my rage. She smiles. What is this? She doesn't say anything. She just keeps smiling at me. Her smile...it's not...taunting me. Somehow it seems to be accepting me... healing me. Without a word, she disappears into her room. Who is she? I rub my eyes. It doesn't matter. She's going to be my Novice Mistress.

Chapter 20

Celine...

This white veil kind of itches, but that's good. Every day, as I watched my father progressively lose his mind, ultimately to die...knowing that this veil awaited me is one of the things that kept me from losing *my* mind. Now I am enjoying a beautiful afternoon at recreation with my new family---three of which happen to be related by blood, one of them being my first Prioress. Not a bad start. The bell rings and everyone starts going back in. I'm on my way, but then I hear the unmistakable voice of Mother Marie de Gonzague, the former Prioress, now Novice Mistress.

"All novices are to remain out here!"

She looks at Thérèse---whom I'm feeling like I barely know lately.

"That means you Sister Thérèse of the Child Jesus!"

Thérèse halts and turns around as the other nuns walk past her. We novices gather in front of Mother Marie de Gonzague in front of the huge crucifix, and are motioned to sit on the ground---charming. Thérèse walks up beside her. Why is she here? Our Novice Mistress addresses us after we're settled.

"Very good. This is Sister Thérèse of the Child Jesus and the Holy Face. She will be assisting me with mentoring you during your novitiate."

Did I just hear right? Mother Marie de Gonzague turns to Thérèse with a sly smirk.

"Sister Thérèse...they're all yours."

She then retires into the convent.

Thérèse looks a bit surprised to be left alone with us. Not nearly as surprised as I am… She sits down on the crucifix's mount, becoming composed, and addresses us.

"Afternoon, Sisters. I hope you're settling in nicely with our community. Along with Mother Marie de Gonzague, I am going to do everything I can to help you learn how Carmelites are to conduct themselves…Sister Genevieve? Are you okay?"

I guess my surprise was a bit too apparent. Wait…did my sister just *not* call me Celine? It's okay. I'll have a little fun with her.

"Yes, Sister or… Mother? I'm fine."

One of my fellow novices snickers a bit---I think her name is Sister Marie of the Trinity---I don't know how to keep up with all of these "Maries." Thérèse gives us both a slightly incredulous look.

"…No, just 'Sister' is fine. I'm not officially the Novice Mistress…"

Sister Marie of the Trinity playfully interrupts.

"…You just have to do all of the dirty work."

We all get a good laugh.

Thérèse appears unfazed. Interesting, the Thérèse I remember would be in tears about now. She just smirks a bit, with a look in her eyes that I have never seen before, and speaks with a tone that quickly silences us.

"Okay, I suppose a good place to start is respect and obedience to your superiors and for that matter to each other. Coming here into Carmel, it is important to realize that we have taken Jesus as our spouse and that His will is represented through our superiors. He speaks to us through them even if their intentions for saying what they do might be motivated by their own selfishness and their orders appear nonsensical to us. Every soul is different and requires different forms of nourishment. What one soul needs another might see as foolish. It is Jesus who inspires our superiors and directs us through them, even if we and our superiors are unaware of it. Our vow of obedience is truly a gift. What better compass can we ask for in doing the will of God? Bearing that in mind: respect Mother Agnes. Respect Mother Marie de Gonzague. Don't gossip about them; don't even think badly about them. Give them the benefit of the doubt, as well as the other Sisters, and each other. We're on the same side. We all belong to Jesus. And we are all pleasing to Him, even if we may not be to each other. If a fellow Sister causes you displeasure, offer to Jesus what is in her that pleases *Him*, and never think more highly of yourself than you do of others."

I really *don't* know her anymore...

"...That's all for today, go tend to your assigned duties."

She quickly stands up and starts walking toward the entrance. I'm a little stunned as I try to get to my feet and see Sister Marie of the Trinity catch up to her and get her attention. Thérèse turns around and looks at her as the other novices begin to pass them. Sister Marie of the Trinity speaks sheepishly to her.

"I'm...really glad we were given to you."

Thérèse smiles and motions her on toward the entrance as I get to my feet. I can't help but agree with my fellow novice---the youngest of us at that. I grab Thérèse's arm.

"Thérèse, I'm sorry. I was just a little caught off guard that my little sister is my Novice Mistress."

"I'm *not* the Novice Mistress."

I scoff. This is too much.

"Oh, come on...if what Mother Marie de Gonzague just did is any indication of what's to come, you may not have the 'title,' but the duty has been put on your shoulders."

"My *only* duty is to offer myself to Jesus in everything I do. This is a responsibility we now share. It is hard to understand, but you must come to realize, *Sister Genevieve*, the unique place we have as nuns. Why do you think we are here? Just to flee from the world? From responsibility? No! We embrace it in a particular way. As spouses of Jesus we have a special place in His Heart when it comes to prayer and sacrifice. There is no gesture of prayer from us too small, even if just a glance to Heaven, that will not make Him cry out with joy! And He is ready to light the world on fire with love from just the slightest inconveniences we offer to Him as sacrifices. Now come on, we're not at Les Buissonnets anymore. It won't help us here to get caught up in long conversations like we used to."

She goes in. I follow. I guess I'll be doing a lot of that in the coming years.

Chapter 21

Thérèse...

The Host touches my tongue. I am set ablaze once more. Why can't we do this every day? Jesus, my Spouse, our Spouse, waits…a willing prisoner in the tabernacle, every day, nonstop, so that He may make tabernacles of us! I feel tears flow down my cheeks as I swallow Him once more, and He in turn swallows me in His love. He is always here in this church, in churches throughout the world…waiting. And how is He treated? With indifference. So few wait with Him, and so many ignore, or even reject. All I can do is offer myself, little though I may be. One might be inclined to think that it is His justice that demands satisfaction, but it is His love!

Mass has ended. I catch up with Mother Agnes. I can tell she is distracted---her adjustment to being Prioress has not come easy.

"Mother, I need to ask you something…"

"What is it Thérèse? I'm kind of in a hurry."

"So many Carmelites have offered themselves to the justice of God, attempting to take upon themselves the wrath justice demands for sin."

"Are you trying to ask me if you can do the same?"

"On the contrary…I wish to offer myself to His merciful love, which I believe is what His justice truly consists of. I want to offer myself simply for the sake of consoling Him in the face of all who reject His love."

"Okay, Thérèse, do what you feel is best."

She hurries off. She doesn't understand, but all I needed was the permission.

Chapter 22

Sister Marie of the Trinity...

It is late and I am tired, but I can't get over how quickly things can turn around. I was on the brink of leaving, and I'm kept in by a simple smile. Her words today were just as powerful. "We're on the same side..." Well, at least the two of us are. That will do. Time for bed.

As I am about to pass by the chapel, I hear words almost being whispered from inside.

"O My God...Most Blessed Trinity...I desire to love You...and make You loved...to work for the glory of Holy Church by saving souls on earth...and liberating those suffering in purgatory. I desire to accomplish Your will perfectly and to reach the degree of glory You have prepared for me in Your Kingdom."

I peak inside. It's her, kneeling in the dark, alone, in front of the Blessed Sacrament. Her back is turned to me. Does she ever stop?

"I desire, in a word, to be a saint, but...I feel my helplessness and I beg You, O my God...to be *Yourself* my sanctity! Since You loved me so much as to give me Your only Son as my Savior *and* my Spouse, the infinite treasures of His merits are mine. I offer them to You with gladness, begging You to look upon me only in the Face of Jesus and in His heart burning with *love*. I offer You, too, all the merits of the saints, in heaven and on earth, their acts of love, and those of the holy angels. Finally, I offer You, O Blessed Trinity, the love and merits of the Blessed Virgin, *my* dear Mother. It is to *her* I abandon my offering, begging her to present it to You. Her Divine Son, my Beloved Spouse, told us in the days of His mortal life: 'Whatsoever you ask the Father in my name *He will give it to you!*' I am *certain*, then, that You will grant my desires. I know, O my God…that the more You want to *give*, the more You make us *desire*. I feel in my heart *infinite* desires and it is with confidence I ask You to come and take possession of my soul."

She pauses and slowly bends over on to all-fours.

"Ah! I cannot receive Holy Communion as often as I desire…but Lord…are You not *all-powerful?* Remain in me as in a tabernacle and never separate Yourself from Your little victim. I want to console You for the ingratitude of the wicked, and I beg of You to take away my 'freedom' to displease You. If through weakness I sometimes fall, may Your divine glance cleanse my soul *immediately*, consuming all my imperfections like the fire that transforms everything into itself. I thank You, O my God, for all the graces You have granted me…especially the grace of making me pass through the crucible of *suffering*. It is with *joy* I shall contemplate You on the Last Day carrying the *scepter* of Your *Cross*. Since You deigned to give me a share in this very precious Cross, I hope in heaven to resemble You and to see shining in my glorified body the sacred stigmata of Your Passion. After earth's Exile, I hope to go and enjoy *You* in the Fatherland, but I do not want to lay up merits for heaven. I want to work for Your Love *alone* with the one purpose of pleasing You, consoling Your Sacred Heart, and saving souls who will love You eternally. In the evening of this life, I shall appear before You with *empty* hands, for I do not ask You, Lord, to count my works. All our justice is stained in Your eyes. I wish, then, to be clothed in Your *own* justice and to receive from Your Love the *eternal* possession of *Yourself.* I want no other *Throne,* no other *Crown* but *You,* my Belovéd! Time is *nothing* in Your eyes, and a single day is like a thousand years. You can, then, in *one instant* prepare me to appear before You."

She begins to rise back up to her knees.

"In order to live in one single act of *perfect* Love…"

I jump a bit as she almost shouts, looking up at the Lord.

"I OFFER MYSELF AS A VICTIM OF HOLOCAUST TO YOUR MERCIFUL LOVE! I want You to consume me *incessantly*, allowing the waves of *infinite* tenderness shut up within You to *overflow* into my soul, and that thus I may become a *martyr* of Your Love, O my God! May this martyrdom, after having prepared me to appear before You, finally cause me *to die* and may my soul take its flight without any delay into the eternal embrace of *Your Merciful Love*. I want, O my Beloved, at *each beat* of my heart to renew this offering to You an *infinite* number of times, until the shadows having disappeared, I may be able to tell You of my love in an *ETERNAL FACE TO FACE!*"

"Sister?"

Did I say that out loud? She tenses and then turns around to face me. I ask the only question that comes to mind.

"What are you doing?"

She smiles, immediately being friendly.

"Praying...what are you doing, Sister Marie of the Trinity? And Sister Marie of the Sacred Heart wonders why I don't just call her Marie."

Funny. I kneel down beside her.

"I was listening...could you teach me that prayer?"

"Later perhaps. I'll need to ask Mother Agnes again...even if she might not know what I'm talking about. Also if *you* want to know it, I suspect Cel---I mean Sister Genevieve will want to know it too. I'll teach it to both of you."

"Where did you learn it?"

"I didn't. It was just in my heart. I felt it burning inside me after I received Communion today."

"I wish I could pray like that. I get carried away by so many distractions when I pray. I have thoughts about people that I would rather not have."

She looks at the tabernacle, smiling reminiscently.

"I often fall asleep when I pray...but I also have a lot of distractions. When I perceive them, I pray for the people who occupy my imagination, and then *they* get to benefit from my distractions."

I can't help but smile. Where does she get these ideas? I change the subject.

"I never thanked you."

"For what?"

"You saved my vocation with just a smile."

She smiles all the more.

"I know all too well what it's like to be treated like an outcast, like I don't belong. I entered Carmel at fifteen. It was difficult, but I knew it was what I was called to do. Not everyone took kindly to my entrance, and seeing you reminded me of that. If I could make it here, so will you."

I don't even think. I find myself hugging her. After a brief moment, I feel her arms around me, as she softly admonishes me.

"Okay…it's getting late."

Part III
Exile's End

Chapter 23

(3 years later...)

Thérèse...

I have to admit, I was disappointed when Mother Agnes was not re-elected. Right now, however, the timing couldn't be better. I woke up this morning to a strange feeling in my side. Before I could even get out of bed, I began coughing violently. It was so bad that it blurred my vision, and I wasn't able to tell right away that my hands were covered in blood.

Good Friday...what a beautiful day to find out that my exile will soon be at an end. This is also why, however, that it is good that Mother Marie de Gonzague is once again Prioress of our community. My older sisters don't have to know right away and start worrying.

Mother Marie de Gonzague is slowly walking down the hall as I get her attention, trying to stay calm.

"I coughed up blood."

Her eyes widen briefly, but her expression remains unchanged.

"You should go to the infirmary and rest."

"I thought you might say that, but we both know what this means. I'm still strong enough, though, to give of myself for Jesus and for souls. Please allow me to continue to observe our Lenten fasting---there are only two more days---and to continue with my duties. I'd like to hold out for as long as possible without drawing attention."

Her expression bears a hint of surprise---at least surprise in the Mother-Marie-de-Gonzague sense of the word.

"As you wish, child. Do what you can. But, I still want you to check in at the infirmary with Sister Marie of the Trinity and let her know. You may keep it quiet otherwise."

***

Sister Marie of the Trinity recently received her black veil and acts now as our infirmarian, which means she attends to the needs of the sick in the community. It would be better if it was still my old Novice Mistress, Sister Marie of the Angels. I say this because Sister Marie of the Trinity has grown close to me over the past few years and I know she will not take this well…but obedience is obedience---I have to tell her. It could be worse… Sister Genevieve has also acted as infirmarian.

I decide to attempt a lighthearted approach and sneak up behind her as she is sweeping in the infirmary.

"Good morning," I say into her ear.

She jumps a bit and, seeing me, smiles as she always does.

"Good morning, yourself! What are you doing here?"

How to say this without sounding too grave?

"Mother Prioress told me to stop by just to let you know about an incident I had this morning that involved me…" I try to brush over the words, "…coughing-up-blood. BUT DON'T WORRY, I'm still allowed to fast and carry out my responsibilities."

Sister Marie of the Trinity's smile gradually gives way to disbelief as she tries process what she just heard.

"…What?"

Here it comes. I sigh. "You heard me."

She begins to tear up in shock. "Sister…? No…you…you can't. Does Mother Agnes know or your other two sisters?"

"Mother Agnes is not the Prioress anymore and I don't want her, or any of my family for that matter, to start worrying about me any sooner than they have to. I've only told you, because you're the infirmarian, and I was ordered to do so. Promise me you'll keep this quiet."

The poor girl reels. I know it's a hard burden I'm putting on her.

"I…promise."

She turns away, drops the broom, and covers her face, while beginning to sob. Everyone knows what typically happens when one has started coughing up blood. I notice the seashell lying on a table. While Sister Marie of the Trinity was still a novice, I gave it to her to try to remedy her tendency to cry so easily. I pick it up and turn her around to face me. I pull her hand down off her face and hold the shell up to it.

"Don't cry. Remember why I gave you this? Any tear you shed goes in here. Don't you cry."

She takes the shell and calms down. At least *that* still works.

Chapter 24

Sister Marie of the Trinity...

This can't be happening! All these years Sister Thérèse has kept me going. She is the only one who has seemed to understand me and be patient with me. I would not be here...I would never have gotten the black veil if not for her! Now out of nowhere...this.

It's all I can do to pick up my bucket and go outside to help with cleaning. It feels way beyond me to pretend like nothing is wrong and I am struck with horror, as I feel the heat outside, and see Sister Thérèse climb up a ladder and begin washing a window, looking exhausted and worn down. This is only the first day of its manifestation and the illness already seems to be killing her! I quickly approach the ladder and try to plead with my friend.

"Sister, I beg you...you're exhausted, please let me finish washing the windows for you!"

She looks down at me, smiling weakly.

"It's okay. I can easily bear this slight fatigue for Him who suffered so much for me on this day."

I can feel tears welling up in my eyes as I plead one last time.

"Please..."

She shakes her head and turns back to her work.

"Go find your shell."

I take off immediately, but not to look for that stupid shell. There is only one person who can stop her that I can talk to without breaking my word. I barge into Mother Marie de Gonzague's cell without any formality, practically yelling at the top of my lungs. Who cares if she might throw me out?

"Mother, this is insane! Please, you have to stop Sister Thérèse of the Child Jesus! She's going to kill herself!"

My good Prioress does not seem the least bit surprised or moved.

"I have already summoned a doctor to come examine her. In the meantime, it is not your concern what I permit or what one of the other Sisters decides to do. Sister Thérèse of the Child Jesus is free to come and tell me herself if she cannot take anymore. Now run along."

I still remember when Sister Thérèse told us before that we should not even *think* badly of our superiors. There are *so* many things I could think right now.

***

My hands are officially tied. All I can do is watch and wait. I've been trying to at least keep an eye on Sister Thérèse from a distance throughout the day. It has not been easy to stomach. She barely made it through Compline. We were all on our knees praying it in the chapel and she was hardly able to chant or stay upright. I don't know how others didn't notice. The closest she came to being discovered was foiled by her stubbornness. We got to a point in the prayer where we all had to stand. She wasn't getting up at first. Sister Marie of the Angels, who was leading the prayer, noticed and motioned for her to get up. I thought this charade might finally end, but then Sister Thérèse forced herself to her feet. Just as she got up, however, the rest of us were going back down to our knees.

Her breviary tumbled out of her hands as she tried to keep herself steady, while going back down. She picked it back up and continued trying to chant with us, and still…no one noticed.

That was just one thing I had to silently watch. I'm following her at a distance now as she slowly approaches her cell in a cold sweat. At least the day is over and she can rest now. As she opens the door, however, she begins coughing and falls to all-fours inside her cell. I rush in and see a puddle of blood expanding on the floor as she coughs.

"Oh God, Sister…!"

I place my hands on her shoulders. After what feels like an eternity she finally stops and all I can hear is her strained breathing. I feel beside myself.

"What do I do? What can I do?"

She changes the subject, while sounding a bit nauseous. I don't know how she can even speak.

"In Carmel…a day without suffering…is a day wasted.…Before I entered Carmel…when I woke up in the morning…I used to think about what the day could possibly have in store for me, happy or troublesome, and if I foresaw only troubles, I got up depressed."

Sister Thérèse pushes herself up and sits on her heels, her chest heaving, her eyes staring off.

"Now it is the opposite. I think only of the pains and sufferings that await me, and I get up so much more joyful and full of courage when I think of the opportunities that I will have to prove my love for Jesus and earn a living for my children, since I am a mother of souls."

Her breathing settles, and she smiles reminiscently, while wiping her bloody lips on her sleeve, and is somehow speaking with more ease, as she removes her veil. Her short blonde hair is soaked with sweat.

"After that I kiss my crucifix, I put it gently at my place on the pillow and while I'm getting dressed, I say to Him… 'Jesus, *you* have worked and wept long enough during the thirty-three years of your life on this poor earth! Today, you rest…It's my turn to fight and to suffer!'"

Sister Thérèse forces herself to her feet but stumbles. I just barely catch her and guide her to her bed. In my arms, she looks at me with a sad and tired expression. Almost like disappointment.

"Please don't go to Mother Prioress on my behalf again. I can assure you that she knows how exhausted I am and that she is inspired by God to let me carry on to the end of my strength."

She closes her eyes, appearing to be drifting off to sleep, but then opens them again.

"I'm going to sleep now, but if you're so anxious to help me, you can aid me with getting all the way into my bed."

I immediately help get her legs onto her bed, and position her head on her pillow. I'm the one who needs comforting, but I try to reassure her.

"Mother Prioress says she's called a doctor. Maybe he can help."

Sister Thérèse just scoffs.

"Look at the blood on the floor. Jesus has chosen the day of His Passion and Death to tell me that He'll be bringing me to Himself soon…"

She goes to sleep without another word.

Chapter 25

Thérèse...

A doctor has arrived at the convent to examine me. It was decided that it was not yet necessary for him to actually enter the convent for this examination, so I have my head between the cloister bars. Prior to this, when the doctor first saw me enter the parlor, he looked surprised. I guess he was expecting me to look a lot worse. Maybe he's disappointed. I'd apologize, but there's a stick in my mouth.

"Say 'awww.'"

He removes the stick.

"I don't see anything out of the ordinary. Are you experiencing any pain at this time?"

"No, it's strange. Yesterday, I was really struggling, but now it's like nothing happened. I am not coughing or anything."

"It's possible that the bleeding you experienced was just a broken blood-vessel in your throat or it might have even come from your nose without you realizing."

Now I'm the one who's surprised.

"My *nose?*"

"It happens. You seem fine now, though, so I wouldn't worry about it."

He then stands up and exits without further word. I withdraw my head from between the bars.

I *wasn't* worried...

***

Sister Marie of the Trinity is waiting for me outside of the visiting parlor. I enter the hall and we begin walking side-by-side. I keep quiet, but I can feel her eyes on me and her anticipation building.

"Well? What did the doctor say?"

I stay casual.

"He said I'm fine. Probably just a nosebleed."

She's taken aback.

"A *nosebleed*!? Sister, you were *coughing up blood*! I *saw* it!"

I shrug.

"Don't be so melodramatic. He also said it could have been a broken blood vessel in my throat or something. The point is, he thinks I'm fine, and until that is proven otherwise, I intend to go about as usual. And, again, don't tell anyone about this. I don't want Mother Agnes or Sister Marie of the Sacred Heart or Sister Genevieve to worry about me. It's been hard enough trying to keep *you* calm."

Sister Marie of the Trinity stops walking. Okay…that was a bit harsh.

"Sister…since I met you after I first entered Carmel, you have become my best friend, as well as a mother to me. You can't blame me for taking the possibility of your death as hard as I did."

I soften and place a hand on her shoulder. I know this has not been easy for her, but I don't want this burden being put on my sisters too, if it can be helped. I gently speak to her.

"Exactly…and that's all the more reason that I don't want *them* to know about this. I'm their little sister, and since my mom's death when I was four, Mother Agnes has taken that place for me. Imagine how hard it would be for her and my other two sisters. Besides, the doctor says I'm fine, so we might as well forget this happened."

The poor girl remains unconvinced.

"I'm still afraid of losing you."

I remove my hand from her shoulder and begin stepping back.

"You don't have to be. Death does not mean separation. For me, it will mean only the beginning of my work. I don't know about you, but I intend to spend my heaven doing good on earth until the end of time. I'm not going anywhere. Even when I die, I will be here on earth working for God and His Church. I promise you. …Now go tell Mother Prioress that I'm okay. It's time to move on."

***

Something is wrong. It is dark and I sit alone in the chapel praying before the Blessed Sacrament. It is Easter Sunday. Two days ago, I was on the brink of death, but as of yesterday I have a clean bill of health. Yet now I feel something moving through my entire being like a poison: nothingness. I begin praying out loud, warm tears are streaming down my face.

"Wheeere did you go? You seemed to tell me that I would be coming Home soon, but now I'm told the opposite. That doesn't bother me---I'm willing to fight and suffer here in this exile for as long as You desire---but... suddenly...I feel nothing. I am overcome with a feeling of torment at just the thought of Heaven. Why does it feel, now, like all that awaits me when I die is nothingness? Are you having me dine now with atheists? To become a *sister* to them in their darkness?"

This could actually be a great opportunity.

"So be it! I will eat with them. You have held me to your chest, thrown me against the wall, and now you seem to have gone to sleep and are ignoring me, just as a child might treat a ball that he is playing with. ...It's okay. Don't worry my belovéd Child Jesus...I won't wake you."

I then feel something unwelcomingly familiar welling up and I double over coughing, the taste of blood in my mouth. Then I hear a voice even more unwelcomingly familiar: Mother Agnes's.

"Thérèse! Oh God..."

Her voice sounds like an echo. I immediately stop coughing and sit up. My sister is already face-to-face with me. I've never seen fear in her eyes until now. I smile at her and make a last effort.

"I'm fine..."

I try to stand, but it's hopeless. I say one last thing before blacking out.

"I can't walk."

Chapter 26

Sister Marie of the Trinity...

Finally, this nightmare charade is over. No more secrets, everyone knows that Sister Thérèse is ill. She lies in bed, half-conscious, in the infirmary flanked by Sister Genvieve and myself. A doctor, Mother Agnes, Sister Marie of the Sacred Heart, and Mother Marie de Gonzague are huddled at a slight distance from us. A more thorough examination has been conducted on Sister Thérèse and I can hear the doctor trying to keep a low tone as he speaks with them.

"She has tuberculosis...and it seems to have already reached an advanced stage. Her right lung has been consumed and I suspect there is gangrene in her intestines."

The only one who visibly reacts to that statement is Sister Marie of the Sacred Heart, but I also see Sister Genevieve's face drop, as she looks over her little sister. Sister Thérèse's reaction, however, surprises us all.

"So much the better..."

She almost sounds amused. The four huddled briefly look back at us and the doctor signals that they should step outside. Mother Prioress looks at me and signals that I should follow. Sister Genevieve stays by Sister Thérèse's side. I exit into the hallway with the others and close the door behind us, while the doctor continues.

"She might only have a few months. Her strength could come and go during that time. If she is able to get around, let her. It would be especially good for her to have time outdoors, but make sure she takes regular nourishment. *No* fasting. Also, have an infirmarian administer pointes de feu for her. That should help cut down on her hemorrhaging. I'll be by to check on her weekly."

The doctor then takes his leave. The four of us are silent for a while and all I can think of is how horrible it will be when Sister Thérèse has to undergo pointes de feu, and will it be by *my* hand? Mother Prioress breaks the silence, ignoring me and addressing the two Martin sisters.

"You two and Sister Genevieve are to care for Sister Thérèse of the Child Jesus. I will also appoint another infirmarian to help as needed."

They nod and go back into the infirmary. I am about to follow, but the Prioress stops me.

"Sister Marie of the Trinity…I am going to assign an *older* infirmarian to assist the Martin sisters as they care for Sister Thérèse of the Child Jesus. You are relieved of your duties here and are to pick up in laundry."

I turn to face her, trying to hide my shock.

"Mother, if you feel I am unfit to help here I assure you…"

"It's not that. You are very young and could be more susceptible should the tuberculosis prove contagious."

This is not happening.

"But…"

"Did you not hear me? You are to begin work in laundry and stay away from Sister Thérèse of the Child Jesus!"

I run to my cell, just before my emotions force their way out of me. I fall to my knees over my bed, muffling my screams and cursing with my pillow. I grab that shell…looking for any consolation I can find. It's not long, however, before I feel it crack in my hands…

Chapter 27

Celine...

Pointes de feu...I don't know who had the crazy idea that somehow plunging red-hot needles into someone's back over and over again would somehow help with tuberculosis, but that's what's about to happen to Thérèse, yet again. Her back is exposed and veil off as she lies hunched over the infirmary bed, waiting for what is to come. There is no fear in her eyes, as I kneel down on the other side of the bed and take her hand--- only a sense of resignation. She smiles as I tell her to keep her eyes on me.

It's good that Sister Marie of the Angels has been assigned as my assistant infirmarian, because I certainly could not do this to my baby sister, and I doubt Sister Marie of the Trinity would have had the stomach for it either. We have been at this for what feels like months. The same day every week as the doctor has prescribed. I've counted over 500 marks on Thérèse's back from this tortuous "treatment." Sister Marie of the Angels has completed her heating of today's needle and stands over Thérèse. I look up at the old nun, knowing I shouldn't hate her for what she's about to do, but I can't quite help it.

Thérèse's jaw tightens in pain as the burning needle pierces the skin of her back and her blood sizzles as it engulfs the needle. The needle is withdrawn and she relaxes. It enters again and her pain is more pronounced. Another time and she is biting the covers of the bed to stifle her screams. The grip of her hand almost crushes mine. All I can do is rest my head on hers and feudally try to comfort her.

It feels like forever before the torture, treatment, whatever, comes to an end. Sister Marie of the Angels drops the needle into a pan of water, causing it to steam. I gently begin to cover Thérèse's back and fasten her scapular back on. As I do, Thérèse actually tries to be humorous.

"Careful Celine...Sister Genevieve---I'd rather not have another incident like when I was a novice."

"What?"

"One day, I was having trouble getting my scapular fastened and another Sister was kind enough to help me. She didn't know, however, that when she fastened my scapular at my shoulder, she had accidently stuck the pin through my skin."

"I'll be careful...you got her to take it out, right?"

"No. I thanked God for it and decided to let it be for a few hours. Looks like that was a better idea than I thought at the time. It was a good warm up for this."

I finish fastening her scapular not knowing whether to feel amused or disturbed by that story. Who is this girl? Where is my little sister who used to bawl her eyes out when she pricked her finger on a thorn?

She slowly pushes herself up with her arms as I support her and gets turned around into a seated position on the bed. She puts her veil back on as Sister Marie of the Angels approaches Thérèse with a cup of milk.

"Here, child, drink this."

An almost nauseous look comes over Thérèse.

"Milk isn't very agreeable for me."

I know she needs the nutrition, though, so I press her.

"Thérèse, right now your *duty* is to be a good patient and accept what is recommended for you. You could think of it as being needed to save *my* life."

Without further hesitation, Thérèse takes the cup and chugs it down. Sister Marie of the Angels looks pleased.

"Good girl. Now, if you can get up the strength, I want you to go for a thirty minute walk outside. The fresh air and exercise should do you some good."

I now wish I had not spoken of duty because then I might be able to stop Thérèse from going on a useless walk that will only drag her down. She doesn't look at Sister Marie of the Angels; she just nods and slowly stands up with my help. She motions for me to stay behind. I only hope she'll make it back in one piece.

Chapter 28

Marie...

I don't know what to make of this. One of my little sisters was made Prioress and another one is going to die. I wish I could take her place. When Mama died, Pauline became a mother to Thérèse. When Pauline entered Carmel, that joy fell to me before my entrance. Mothers should not outlive their children. It shouldn't be this way...

I'm out in the garden trying to not be too distracted by these thoughts as I go about my work. I look up and see Thérèse walking slowly, trudging along by herself, looking drained and dragged down. Her condition must be much worse than last week. Given our position in relation to the infirmary, I know she has not been walking for even five minutes. This nonsense about fresh air and exercise needs to stop. I see her fall to one knee while throwing up a white liquid and I immediately drop my rake and begin running toward her. As I get closer, I hear what sounds like laughter. Is she losing her mind? I shout at her.

"Thérèse! What are you doing?"

"Don't worry. That was just some milk that didn't agree with me."

I help her get seated on the large rock she's kneeling beside.

"You shouldn't be out here walking around like this anymore, Thérèse. You're exhausted and it's not helping you."

She smiles weakly.

"It's true, but you know what gives me strength? ...I'm walking for a missionary. I think that over there, far away, one of them is perhaps exhausted in his apostolic endeavors, and...to lessen his fatigue...I offer mine to God."

Thérèse forces herself up and keeps walking. How unknown she has been!

***

I cannot believe how much Thérèse has been taken for granted in this monastery and in our family. Though I always loved her deeply, I've only seen her as a mere child, but the wealth and wisdom that God has planted in her heart...*I'm* the child! I have to get Pauline in on this. It won't do any good for me to talk to Mother Marie de Gonzague on my own.

I knock and find Pauline sitting at her desk with her arms folded, looking at me with a sad expression as I enter her cell. I'll let her talk a little while.

"Are you okay...'Mother'?"

Pauline smiles at me with melancholy.

"I was trying to get some work done, but I got distracted thinking of Thérèse. I was regretting something I did that hurt her when she put on a play a couple of years ago to celebrate my feast day as Prioress; you remember? The one about the flight into Egypt?"

I nod and keep silent as she goes on.

"I found the play to be too long and perhaps wearisome to the community, and of course you remember the spectacle I made interrupting and shutting it down before Thérèse and the other novices could finish. She was so humiliated...even though she never betrayed it when around others, always maintaining that peaceful demeanor we've come to take for granted. I might not have even known of her humiliation had Celine not told me she spotted Thérèse hiding herself while trying to wipe away tears. I've looked over the script of that play since then, and it really wasn't *that* bad. I was just too concerned about what the older Sisters in our community might think of me as Prioress for allowing it to go on, with its drinking bouts and 'modern' melodies. And I wasn't even re-elected. Serves me right, I guess..."

I hunch down coming eye to eye with Pauline.

"You may have become a 'Mother' in our community, but you're still my little sister. Let go of that regret and any regret you may have in her regard. Thérèse certainly would not want you to carry it, especially now."

Pauline touches my face and snickers a little.

"I'm sorry. You came to see me and here I am telling you about *my* problems."

I sit on Pauline's bed.

"You know, our Thérèse is likely going to leave us soon, but I feel there is a lot she could still leave behind."

"What do you mean?"

"I mean that while there is still time, there is something she should be writing..."

***

"Write what?"

Thérèse asks as she coughs up blood in the infirmary. Celine wipes Thérèse's mouth as Pauline continues speaking while slowly pacing.

"Whatever you can think of. I would suggest beginning with your childhood memories, perhaps. But also, we really want to know as much detail as possible about your relationship with God. It will make for a good memento of you for our family to hold on to. I talked this over with Mother Prioress and she has agreed to allow it. I think it would be wise for you to begin as soon as possible."

I can tell by the look on Thérèse's face that she doubts anything will come of this, but as I predicted, her zest for obedience continues to prevail even as her illness worsens.

"Got a pen?"

Chapter 29

Sister Marie of the Trinity...

Three months. I've been cut off for *three months*. Why? I'm too young? Maybe they're too old! How do we even know, if Sister Thérèse is in fact contagious, that *older* people won't be more vulnerable around her? Her sisters, particularly Sister Genevieve, aren't what I would call *older*. So how do we know that *they* won't catch the tuberculosis? Maybe that's Mother Prioress's intention. Thin out the abundance of Martin sisters we have in the Community. Why not have me go with them, then? Sister Thérèse is family to *me*!

My shell may have been busted, but I still have this spin top that I've been playing with all day. Hey, if I'm such a child, why not act my age? I abruptly stop, though, as I hear the voices of Mother Agnes and Sister Marie of the Sacred Heart passing by my cell. Just because I can't be around her, doesn't mean I can't get information. I can easily hear Mother Agnes as I follow at a distance.

"Thérèse has made good progress in her writings, but the doctor says her condition is worsening. Her other lung is beginning to be consumed and she is not supposed to walk anymore. We're having to use Papa's old wheelchair to take her outside. It might just be a matter of weeks."

That's the last time I will ever eavesdrop. I can't take much more of this. I run outside. I don't know where I'm going, but as I move down the trail, I see Sister Thérèse sitting in her father's old wheelchair under a chestnut tree, working on her manuscripts of which I've been hearing rumors. She looks up and, noticing me, smiles and motions for me to come over to her.

I feel like a knife has been driven into my heart. She wants to see me and I have to tell her no.

"I can't! Someone will see us and I've been forbidden!"

I tearfully run off and enter the Grotto of the Holy Face, falling to all fours before His image and I begin weeping uncontrollably. After what could have only been a few moments, I look up and can scarcely believe my eyes as I make out through my tears Sister Thérèse seated on a stump next to me. She lovingly looks down at me.

"I have *not* been forbidden *to come to you*, and even though I should die of it, I want to console you."

Is this real? I rise to my knees. I can barely speak.

"How did you…?"

Before I can finish, Sister Thérèse embraces me and I begin crying into her chest. I start to calm down, and then Sister Thérèse releases me and wipes the tears off of my face.

"My shell broke…"

She just smiles. It's not long, however, before she begins trembling, in a cold sweat, struggling to hold herself up as her fever worsens. I come to my senses and plead with her.

"Sister, you're trembling and burning up with fever. Please, we have to get you back to your wheelchair."

She looks at me with a weak, but determined smile, while continuing to tremble.

"Yes…but not until you have laughed for me."

I wonder if the fever is affecting her sanity, but I don't hesitate in obeying. It's not long, however, before I shout at her.

"CAN WE GO NOW?"

She touches my face and nods. I quickly put one of her arms over my shoulders and together we walk back over to the wheelchair. I get her seated. She closes her eyes and crosses her arms over her chest as she continues trembling. She can't stay out here.

"I'm taking you back to the infirmary."

I quickly get behind Sister Thérèse's wheelchair and begin rolling her up the trail leading back to the convent.

***

I've gotten Sister Thérèse back in her bed and she's asleep. Sister Genevieve, however, is continuing to barrage me with questions.

"Say that again?"

"I don't know---it was like she just appeared out of nowhere. In any case, it seems to have greatly weakened her. We need to keep an eye on her at all times so she doesn't overdo it again. There's no telling how much more she can take before…"

I'm frozen by Mother Marie de Gonzague's voice.

"Sister Marie of the Trinity…was I not clear the last time we spoke?"

"Mother, I couldn't help it. Sister Thérèse…"

"No excuses. Just leave. I'll deal with you later."

Sister Genevieve tries to intercede.

"Mother, if it weren't for Sister Marie of the Trinity, my little sister would be dead right now."

Mother Prioress is not impressed. I wonder if she ever is…

"Your little sister is going to be dead anyway. I will not needlessly risk her taking others along with her."

Sister Genevieve tenses in anger, which is betrayed by her eyes, as she tightly closes her mouth to contain her outrage. Sister Thérèse weakly speaks up from her bed, lifting her head and gasping for air as she does so.

"It's okay…Mother…I…made…God… promise…no one…would… catch…this…from me."

Her head falls back on the pillow as she coughs up blood. Sister Genevieve rushes to Sister Thérèse's side and wipes the blood off of her mouth. Mother Prioress appears frustrated, but at the same time resigned. Perhaps she doesn't want there to be further drama around Sister Thérèse. Or maybe now it doesn't seem like it's such a bad idea to her that I do in fact die with her…if that's even possible.

"I suppose I'll leave you *Martin* sisters to your own affairs. Sister Marie of the Trinity…do what you please. But you put yourself at risk."

I don't hesitate.

"I'm willing to take that chance if you will *permit* it."

She briefly regards me with a smirk and then exits. My body relaxes with her departure. A huge weight has been lifted off my shoulders. I turn to my adopted family.

"What can I do?"

Chapter 30

Celine...

I remember peeking in on a conversation between my baby sister and Pauline. They were sitting in her room one night and Thérèse was already, at four years old, in the habit of pouring out her heart to Pauline, *and* was already set on being a nun. She was rambling to Pauline with childish determination.

"I will be a religious in a cloister because Celine wants to go there, and, then, also, Pauline, I must learn how to read to children, don't you see? But I will not conduct class for them because this would bore me too much. Celine will do it. I will be Mother; I'll walk all day in the cloister, and then I'll go with Celine; we'll play in the sand and with our dolls..."

I could tell Pauline was having to force herself not to laugh, as she tried gently to help Thérèse see things realistically.

"You think then, dear Thérèse, that you'll talk all day long; do you know that you will have to keep silent?"

This did nothing to break her enthusiasm.

"True... Ah! what a pity! I will say nothing..."

"What will you do then?"

"That's no problem; I'll pray to good Jesus. But what can I do to pray to Him without saying anything? I don't know, and who will show me since I will be Mother? Tell me!"

Pauline couldn't help but smile, but kept from laughing, since Thérèse was obviously dead serious. They were silent for a few moments, and then Thérèse smiled mischievously and suddenly spoke up, throwing her tiny arms in the air.

"What of it, my little Pauline, it's not worth tormenting myself already, I'm too little, don't you see, and when I'll be big like you and Marie, I will be told what to do before entering the cloister!"

Then Pauline started to laugh.

"That's it dear baby."

She then kissed Thérèse on her cheeks and forehead.

"Now it's late; let's get you to bed."

Thérèse is in bed now…but we never would have imagined it being like this. I've been at her bedside for months and months, and her agony just gets worse and worse. This is proving to be a particularly long night. I haven't left her side, but others have been coming and going in shifts. Pauline is here now, praying desperately. I can only sit here feeling helpless as Thérèse gasps for air in agony. The way she's rambling now, as she writhes in the bed, I'm not even sure if she is aware of her surroundings.

"No I musn't talk…But…I believed…I love you so much…I'm going to be good…"

She pauses seeming to have a brief moment of clarity and faces Pauline, who is still praying. She speaks to Pauline as if she pities her.

"Oh, little mother…"

Before she can continue, the suffocating resumes and Thérèse cries out while facing the ceiling, and continuing to gasp.

"…My God! …have pity on your little… girl!… I… can…no longer…even…speak…to you! Oh if only one knew! …If I didn't love God! …Yes, but…"

Thérèse passes out. Pauline stops praying and raises her head, her eyes red with tears. I quickly place my hand on Thérèse's forehead and then raise her wrist, checking for a pulse. I gesture to Pauline that Thérèse is still here. She sighs.

Sister Marie of the Trinity walks in, as I lay Thérèse's wrist down, looking at me with worry on her face.

"Sister Genevieve, is she…?"

"No…just passed out…"

Pauline tiredly weighs in.

"Mercifully, I suppose…"

I know what's she's thinking. It's not that we want our little sister to die, but…God, will this suffering never end? Sister Marie of the Trinity only seems relieved, as she places a hand on Pauline's shoulder.

"Well, this is my hour. I'll take over, Mother. You get some rest."

Pauline, a look of resigned sorrow in her eyes, nods and then rises. As she is walking away and Sister Marie of the Trinity is taking her seat, Thérèse suddenly wakes up and cries out loudly.

"AGNE! AGNE!"

Sister Marie of the Trinity looks curiously at Pauline as she turns around.

"Don't worry, that's just something she says sometimes to try alleviate the suffocation."

I smile.

"She'll also say, from time to time, 'Oh là là!'"

Thérèse mimics me like a parrot.

"Oh là là!"

At least she still has some humor. Maybe she'll get a break from suffocating at least for a little while. But when Pauline steps out and the door closes behind her, Thérèse pitifully cries out in a sort of whimpering tone. She then immediately bangs the back of her head on her pillow, scolding herself.

"Why do I do that?"

Sister Marie of the Trinity sadly sits back in her chair and laments.

"I can't believe you're having to suffer like this. Why must life be so sad?"

Thérèse is quick to respond.

"No…life is not sad. If you were to say that exile is sad, then I might agree with you. But life can only truly be attributed to that which is without end. Heaven. And life is happy…*very* happy."

Sister Marie of the Trinity sighs.

"You know, I'm scared to think what it is like to stand before our Judge after we die, and He asks why He should let us into Heaven."

A look of reminisce comes over Thérèse.

"There's a story I like about a king who sets out on a hunt with his dogs. The dogs pick up the scent of a little white rabbit in a field and begin their pursuit. The rabbit tries to run away but finds itself at the edge of a cliff as the king catches up and his dogs are ready to pounce. Just before they do, however, the rabbit bounds back quickly and jumps into the arms of the king. The king is so moved by the rabbit's act of confidence that he takes it into his castle, cherishes it as his own, and allows no harm to come to it. For me the dogs represent the claims of God's divine justice and the only place we can flee to for refuge is His arms. When I die, I do not believe that God will simply be standing at the gates of Heaven waiting for me to tell Him why He should let me in, since He already knows our hearts as we die…but if such were the case…I would not say anything…I would simply leap into His arms, and the rest would be up to Him. I would do this even if I had every imaginable sin on my conscience. It is not because God has preserved me from mortal sin by his anticipating mercy and love that I go to Him with confidence, but because I know that in His mercy and love, any multitude of sins can be consumed in the twinkling of an eye, like a drop of water thrown into a blazing furnace."

Sister Marie of the Trinity smiles.

"Even with all this suffering your soul is full of light. Perhaps you can even see through the veil that divides Heaven and earth."

Thérèse scoffs in disagreement.

"Veil? More like a wall."

"I don't understand."

"Pick up my journal and look for a folded piece of paper that's inserted in it."

She complies and, finding the paper, unfolds it.

"It's the Apostle's Creed."

"Look closer."

A look of shock erupts on Sister Marie of the Trinity's face.

"It's written in blood!"

"My blood…"

That even surprises me.

"When did you do this?"

"My confessor recommended I write out the Creed. When I got around to it, I decided to use the blood I've been coughing up."

Sister Marie of the Trinity is still staring at it.

"What's this about?"

"At the time of that Good Friday which announced the coming end of my earthly exile, I was enjoying a faith that was living and clear. Thinking of Heaven filled me with so much joy that I could scarcely fathom there were actually people who did not believe, who did not have faith… the only source of real and pure joys. I reasoned that they must be speaking against their own inner convictions, that deep down they cannot really believe that there is no Heaven where God awaits them to be their eternal reward. In the days following the onset of this illness, however…God has allowed my soul to be invaded by the thickest darkness…"

She tears up as she continues.

"…And now I feel dead inside and the thought of Heaven torments me. Satan taunts me with it. He says 'You are dreaming about the light, about a country fragrant with the sweetest perfumes; you are dreaming about the eternal possession of the Creator of all things. You believe that you will walk out of this fog that surrounds you!?"

Thérèse can barely contain her emotions as she finishes.

"Dream on! Dream on! Rejoice in death which will give you not what you hope for, but even deeper night, the night of nothingness!"

She begins weeping in agony. I take her hand. I had no idea. All this time she has been physically suffering the way she has and this is what she's been feeling on the inside, while still exhibiting so much joy? Sister Marie of the Trinity looks equally incredulous as she holds up Thérèse's journal.

"But the manuscripts you've been writing and the poetry…!"

Thérèse begins laughing through her tears.

"To live of love is not to fix one's tent
On Thabor's height and there with Thee remain!
It is to climb our Calvary with strength nigh spent
And count the heavy cross our truest gain!"

She composes herself, and looks back at Sister Marie of the Trinity, smiling as she resumes speaking normally.

"When I sing of the happiness of Heaven, of the eternal possession of God, I feel no joy in this, for I sing simply what I *want* to believe. That is how faith persists. Believing even when we feel nothing. My soul is wrapped in darkness. I feel alone and abandoned by God, but *I have abandoned myself to Him*, and because of that, I am at peace. If I didn't have faith, I'd have killed myself by now without hesitation. It's hard to explain, but faith has helped me to see this trial as a *grace*. I've even gotten through the horror I felt at being prevented by this illness from receiving Jesus in the Eucharist. Everything is grace, and anything I suffer can be offered to God and used for good, not only for myself, but for others, even if we never meet, and even if we are never aware of it."

Sister Marie of the Trinity blushes.

"I cannot begin to fathom your courage…much less imitate it."

Thérèse just smiles.

"You are complaining about something that should cause you the *greatest* happiness. Where would your merit be, if you could fight only when you *feel* courage? What does it matter if you have none, provided that you act as if you do! When you feel too weak to pick up a ball of yarn and you do it anyway for love of Jesus, you have more merit than if you had accomplished something much more important in a moment of fervor. Instead of being sad when you get to feel your weakness, *rejoice* that God is providing you with the opportunity to save a greater number of souls for Him!"

Sister Marie of the Trinity still looks discouraged.

"What good will a ball of yarn do anyone?"

Thérèse laughs gently.

"Oh dear, do you not remember that one Easter we were trying to have a procession, but couldn't get our candles lit? You, however, found one of our oil lamps that was almost extinguished and held your candle to it. Your candle was lit, and with that, everyone's candles in our convent were lit, and an infinity of others could have been lit. But it was from that little lamp that it began. And so it is with one simple act of love. All it takes is the *smallest*…"

Before Thérèse can finish, our oldest sister suddenly barges in, looking like she just woke up. Why is she here so soon?

"Marie?"

Thérèse gives me a look. Wow, even now? I clear my throat.

"I mean…Sister Marie of the Sacred Heart, what are you doing here this early?"

She answers through a yawn.

"Must've lost track of the time. Well, I'm here anyway. Sister Marie of the Trinity might as well go…"

She looks hesitant, but lovingly touches Thérèse's arm and exits. Marie takes her place and sleepily regards Thérèse with a smile as she picks up a cup of water off the nearby table.

"Here, I'm sure you could use some water."

"Why? My mouth is not dry."

This time I give *her* a look. Thérèse nods and takes the cup. I decide to take a break and leave her with Marie. This was a mistake, because when I get back after maybe an hour or so from napping, Marie is asleep in her chair and Thérèse is still holding the cup, her hands trembling with growing fatigue. I don't hesitate.

"Thérèse what are doing!? Give me that!"

Before I get there, Marie wakes up and quickly takes the cup from Thérèse.

"You should have woken me up!"

"I thought you could use the rest."

"How long were you holding it?"

"It doesn't matter…"

Marie looks at me with frustration.

"I can't do this…you think you can look after her alone?"

I smile.

"Thought you'd never ask."

She scoffs.

"Good night."

Alone at last. Thérèse and I just sit for a while silently regarding each other. Once the bright four-year-old who would not be stopped, and now this…

"You're really dying aren't you? I don't know how I'll be able to go on without you when you leave."

Thérèse smiles reassuringly.

"Well then you have nothing to worry about, because I *won't* leave."

"What, you won't go to Heaven?"

"I didn't say that…but I won't leave you either."

"How is that possible?"

"With God, all things are possible. Is it really so hard to believe that one can enjoy the vision of God in Heaven, while at the same time, serving Him here on earth, and helping those still suffering here? My death will only mean the beginning of my work. When I die, I will travel with missionaries, watch over my family here and elsewhere, provide support for priests and those studying to be priests, and, if God allows, I will even perform miracles to bring consolation and healing; all while being set ablaze with the love and vision of God. I will love Him like He has never been loved before, and yet I will also work here on earth until the end of time. Otherwise, it would not be Heaven for me. Our greatest desires come from Him, and He would not have given me this desire, if He did not wish to fulfill it. After all, from the bosom of the beatific vision, do God's angels not watch over us? And we are to be raised *higher* than the angels!"

"Well…for now, you are here as you are, and should rest."

Thérèse smiles and closes her eyes. I guess she still won't be stopped.

Chapter 31

Thérèse continues to surprise me. She has been suffering for more than a year and a half, intermittently on the brink of death, and now she is sitting up in her bed, looking well. Pauline and I are sitting beside her feeling dumbfounded. Thérèse gives us a knowing look. This up and down has played with *her* mind as well.

Mother Marie de Gonzague enters the infirmary and regards Thérèse with surprise.

"Well...look at you up and about. I can't remember the last time I've seen you be able to actually sit up in bed."

Thérèse smiles.

"I feel a lot of strength today. I guess I'm not going to die. I might have months, maybe years! I'd like to go Home as soon as possible, but if it brings the Good God more pleasure for me to remain here, then so be it. I would gladly bear the greatest sufferings possible until the age of eighty, or whatever, if it would only make Him smile just once."

"Perhaps, there would be more for you to gain from such a journey than you think."

Thérèse shrugs.

"I hold nothing in my hands. Everything I have, everything I merit is for the Church and for souls. Even if I *were* to live to eighty, I would always be as poor as I am now."

Thérèse's breathing suddenly becomes heavier and her eyes widen as she coughs up blood. I wipe her face as Mother Prioress rushes closer to Thérèse.

Thérèse looks at her mischievously.

"It might be God's pleasure that I not have to prove that."

A look of agony erupts on Thérèse's face, as she looks down and wraps her arms around her chest, gasping for breath. I stand up and back away, feeling a sudden horror. Is this it? Mother Marie de Gonzague sits in my place beside Thérèse on her bed. There's an expression on the Prioress's face like she's seen this before. Her voice is quiet and sober.

"Sister Genevieve…"

What does she want with me all of the sudden?

"Summon the community here at once…"

I race out of the room. I can't take this anymore. One minute she's dying, then the next she's fine, and the next she's dying again. Something feels different about this one, though. That look on the Prioress's face…

I make it to the bell and start ringing it with all of my might. I start to hear doors opening and closing and see the other Sisters heading toward the infirmary. I kind of wonder if Thérèse would actually want this much company as she dies.

I sprint back to the infirmary, as the bell continues to swing wildly, and I find that I can't even get back to Thérèse's bed because of the crowd. A number of the Sisters kneel around Thérèse's bed and begin praying. Marie pulls up a chair beside Pauline, and places her hand on one of Thérèse's legs. All I can do is look on from the entrance. Thérèse is still choking and gagging on her own blood, but manages to speak again to the Prioress.

"Is this it, Mother? 'The Agony?' Am I going to die?"

Mother Prioress doesn't try to dodge it.

"Yes, child. But it may be prolonged a while longer."

Typical.

Thérèse gasps, while almost laughing.

"So much the better! Let it be as long as *He* wants it!"

Thérèse lays down on her side, facing Pauline, with her arms still crossed and continuing to heave in agony. She coughs up blood, staining the linens her face is pressed against. When Sister Marie of the Trinity sees this, while on her knees, she curls up into a ball.

Still on her side, Thérèse elevates her head slightly off of the bed, looking up at Pauline, and the two hold hands as Thérèse struggles to speak.

"No…I could…never have believed it possible…to have suffered… so much!"

She smiles at Pauline and almost laughs as she continues. "...Never... never...I can...explain it...only by...the ardent thirst...I had...to save souls!"

Pauline looks at Thérèse with a sense of shock as tears begin to pool in her eyes. Thérèse's eyes widen as she lays her head back down. Her mouth opens wide as she unsuccessfully tries to breathe in air, unable to make any further sound, and her face turns a bluish pale. Soon Thérèse is still, her eyes wide open and her mouth beginning to relax. I can see that Thérèse's hand, held by Pauline, has also turned blue. It looks like it's over...

After a moment of silence, however, Thérèse suddenly takes a deep gasping breath as she abruptly sits up, causing our two sisters and the Prioress to reel back in surprise. As Thérèse gazes in front of her, there is an expression of sweet nostalgia on her face, as if seeing a long lost love for the first time in many years, her eyes gradually filling with tears of joy.

"Oh I love Him...My God...I love...You."

Thérèse then gasps and reels her head back as though she has just been stabbed. There is an expression of complete ecstasy on her face. As she gazes, a change comes over her face which gradually returns to its natural color, appearing full of life, and looking very young. She looks at me and I feel a knife go through my heart, as she slowly closes her eyes and gently lies back as Pauline, with a look of confusion, lightly catches her and guides her down. Thérèse is laid down in the bed with her eyes closed and her lips forming the slightest hint of smile, as though she were sleeping in the arms of her Beloved. Mother Marie de Gonzague looks at Thérèse curiously, as Pauline, in tears, places her hand on Thérèse's forehead, and Marie weeps in agony.

I have to see the sky. More happened here than just her dying. Maybe I can see her on her way...I run outside hoping to see her, but it's pouring down rain. The thunder and lightning taunt me. I scream at the top of my lungs.

"WHY CAN'T THE STARS BE OUT!?"

I sink to a fetal position against a column, beginning to weep. I bury my head in my arms and knees. Somehow, in spite of my weeping, I become aware that it is quiet around me. I look up to see that, in just seconds, the storm has stopped, the clouds are gone, and all that remains are an array of stars.

Epilogue

Sister Marie of the Trinity...

I wondered for a while how I would be able to go on after the loss of my friend, my mother...but over the years I have become more and more aware that I have not actually lost her. Even now, as I stand over her grave, I feel as though she is standing beside me. I'm here with two of her blood sisters and with another Sister who I haven't gotten to know too well, Sister St. Vincent de Paul. I kneel down and place some fresh roses at the foot of her cross and read over the inscription for the millionth time.

Sister Thérèse of the Child Jesus and the Holy Face

1873-1897

"I will spend my heaven doing good on earth."

I stand back up. It still hurts, but "so much the better." Sister Marie of the Sacred Heart breaks the silence.

"It seems the words on her grave are coming true. Mother Agnes just told me that a case has been opened in the Vatican for Thérèse to be named a saint."

I hear Sister St. Vincent de Paul scoff.

"Why? What'd she do?"

And God smiled...

Appendix I

John D. Wright

Saint Thérèse of Lisieux

(Lecture note: This lecture was first written and presented in February of 2014. Updates have since been added. Clearly there is a lack of citation. Everything is derived from a combination of Wikipedia [primarily used for the "Background"] and things I remember off the top of my head from my approximately seven years of reading about and having interest in Thérèse [and never, until less than a week before giving this lecture for the first time, having in mind to write anything like this]. The items I have read and am drawing from, whether knowingly or unknowingly, include *Story of a Soul, Saint Therese* (sic.) *of Lisieux: Her Last Conversations, Thérèse of Lisieux and Marie of the Trinity, My Sister Saint Thérèse, Maurice and Thérèse*, and *Therese* (sic.) *and Lisieux*, just to name the big ones I remember off the top of my head. I might also include information I happen to remember from daily devotionals to her, conversations I have had about her or just random stuff I have stumbled upon on the internet that could have come from Facebook for all I know. If I specifically quote something and was able to find and locate where that information came from that I remembered, then I try to cite it, though I might not always be successful. I do not, however, allow a lack of remembrance of specific sources to compromise the dissemination of whatever I remember about Thérèse that I can't remember specific sources for. While I was writing with the intention of presenting this material in a lecture, this is by no means a professional dissertation. I'm basically just talking about a woman I have really come to love.)

I. Background

Born Marie-Françoise-Thérèse Martin on Rue Saint-Blaise, Alençon, in the French Department of Orne on January 2, 1873. Her parents were Louis and Zélie Martin, who are also canonized saints of the Catholic Church. Zélie died of breast cancer when Thérèse was four years old. Thérèse had four older sisters, Marie, Pauline, Leonie, and Celine. All of the Martin sisters entered religious life, Celine being the last after Louis's death. That's right, Thérèse entered before one of her older sisters. She was only fifteen when she joined the Carmelite Order in Lisieux. Her entrance did not come easy, which is understandable given her age. She had the full support of Celine and Louis, as well as her motherly sister, Pauline, who was already in Carmel under the name Sister Agnes. Her oldest sister---who was also her Godmother---in Carmel, Sister Marie of the Sacred Heart, was not so supportive[1], nor was the Carmelite Superior, Father Delatroëtte. Louis took Thérèse to their Bishop, Flavien Hugonin, who was gracious to Thérèse, and edified by Louis's support, but nevertheless said that further deliberation would be required.

Thérèse then journeyed on pilgrimage to Rome, in 1887, with Louis and Celine, and this ultimately culminated in an audience with Pope Leo XIII. Thérèse boldly, though she had been told to keep silent in his presence, asked him to grant permission for her to enter Carmel at the age of fifteen. The Pope was very warm to Thérèse, and after advising her to follow the discretion of her superiors, assured her that she would enter if it was God's will. In April of 1888, Thérèse finally was able to enter the Carmel of Lisieux as Sister Thérèse of the Child Jesus, later adding "and the Holy Face" to her name.

While in Carmel, her father suffered from cerebral arteriosclerosis ---it basically involves strokes.

They caused him to have hallucinations and eventually killed him. After his death, Celine entered Carmel as Sister Genevieve of the Holy

---

[1] I cannot remember how I got that impression, possibly from *The Passion of St. Thérèse*, but letters of correspondence that I've read lately from Sister Marie of the Sacred Heart herself seem to indicate the opposite (added April 2, 2015).

Face,[2] in 1894. Interestingly enough, Thérèse was given charge of providing her older sister, as well as other novices, with spiritual guidance, having *unofficially* been made the Novice Mistress. On September 30, 1897, at the age of 24, Thérèse died an extremely painful death from tuberculosis. The end.

II. Why Thérèse?

That doesn't sound like much of a background, does it? So how does a girl who enters a secluded and closed off life as a religious at the age of 15 and die at 24, and is really only known at the time to her small community of Sisters, many of them who were not too closely affiliated with her, become a canonized saint, Doctor of the Church, and a patroness of missionaries? When talks of her cause to sainthood arose, one of the Sisters in her community even said "Why? She didn't do anything."

I'm still trying to wrap my head around that myself. I have absolutely fallen in love with Thérèse, yet I have difficulty explaining why. Thérèse, herself, wanted to be unknown and forgotten. However, her sister, Pauline, was elected prioress during Thérèse's time, and she and Marie got the idea to have Thérèse write about her life and her spirituality, intended to be a sort of souvenir for their family. Thérèse would have never written something like that on her own initiative, but she could not refuse an order from her *now* Mother Prioress. This is where we get her autobiography, *Story of a Soul*, one the most famous works ever in Catholic spirituality. It consists of three Manuscripts. Manuscript A, is the longest and I would say most autobiographical. In it she describes her childhood, her struggle to enter Carmel at her young age, and her experiences in Carmel until around 1895, two years before she died. Something especially worth noting in Manuscript A is that it reveals that she acted as a spiritual mother since she was a teenager.

When she was that age, a man named Henri Pranzini brutally murdered two women and a twelve year old girl. He was captured and slated for execution. Thérèse followed his story through her local newspaper. What

---

[2] This was the name she ultimately took, having had two other names prior (added August 23, 2015).

concerned her most about it was that he was not showing any repentance for what he had done and was refusing to go to Confession. She took it upon herself to pray for him, referring to him as her child, and trusting that God would not allow him to be damned. Right before he was executed, Pranzini requested to be given a crucifix and he kissed the wounds of Christ. Thérèse was ecstatic to read this news. Think about that: this man, so that he could steal jewelry, brutally cuts the throats of two women and a little girl. Monstrous, savage…yet Thérèse, a teenager, refers to him as her *child* and, while I'm sure it can be held that she understood the brutality of Pranzini's actions, her primary focus was his salvation. How many teenaged girls would be prone to think this way?

She addresses Manuscript B to her oldest sister, Marie. This manuscript is the shortest and gives a taste of Thérèse's theology. It gives a feel for the depth of Thérèse's desire to please God, as she relates a draw to the vocations of warrior, priest, apostle, doctor, and martyr. She comes to the conclusion that no one vocation is enough to make her feel satisfied in serving God. She read from Paul in *1ˢᵗ Corinthians* that not all can be prophets, apostles, doctors, etc., and as she continues reading she comes upon where Paul describes that all these offices are nothing without love. So while she does not at first see herself in any of the members of the Church, she realizes that her place is in the heart of the Church, that her vocation is love and that embraces all things.

There was a sense of urgency with Manuscript C. Thérèse was dying of tuberculosis, and her sisters felt there was more that needed to be written. The prioress before her sister had been re-elected, and so Pauline no longer had the authority to order Thérèse to write more. However, Pauline was able to talk it over with the current Prioress and Thérèse was ordered to continue her work. Manuscript B gives an overview of the nature of Thérèse's vocation; Manuscript C, on the other hand, gives an overview of how she lived it.

She relates times where she goes out of her way to be inconvenienced, humiliated, or just flat annoyed for the sake of love and to participate in Jesus's redeeming work for souls. There was a Sister in the community that annoyed Thérèse in every way possible---Thérèse would make it a point to be around her and pleasant toward her, to the extent that this Sister thought Thérèse, for whatever reason, was attracted to her. Thérèse was blamed for things that she didn't do, like breaking a vase or causing a commotion outside of her sick Prioress's door---she would take it without trying to defend or justify herself, imitating Jesus in His Passion.

Thérèse, without being asked, would help an elderly and demanding nun get to the refectory, which is the name of the room where Religious eat. Then, seeing this nun struggle to cut her bread, Thérèse would cut it for her and then smile at her. This nun would be bickering the whole way to the refectory, but after seeing Thérèse's smile, her disposition completely changed---that smile made her day. The old nun wasn't the only one; I can't remember if this is in *Story of a Soul,* but I read one account where Thérèse noticed a particular Sister was having a really bad day. At the end of the day, before going into her cell, Thérèse waited outside until this particular nun was passing by, then Thérèse gave the nun her best smile, before going into her cell, not saying a word, and that smile, alone, completely turned things around for the nun.

There is also an account where Thérèse is trying to pray and someone behind her is making a distracting noise or she's doing laundry and someone is unconsciously splashing dirty water in her face---Thérèse would not try to stop them, but would actually embrace what was being done to her, not wanting to miss any opportunity to participate in Christ's redeeming work in any little way that was made available to her. Hence we have her famous "Little Way." She observed the Little Way to the point of hardcore. A simple example is the end of Manuscript C. As I said, she was dying when she wrote this, and she literally wrote until she could not hold her pencil anymore. That is why Manuscript C ends with "…" She died three months later.

Accounts related outside of *Story of a Soul* demonstrate the extremes of just *how* powerful Thérèse was in the Little Way. Before I go into detail, though, I just want to make a little disclaimer. What I am about to describe might very well make Thérèse sound like she was taken in madness. What needs to be kept in mind, however, is that Thérèse viewed *everything* she experienced in Carmel, small or big, as a continuous offering to Jesus, whom she refers to as her Spouse. Her greatest desire was to participate in His suffering for the salvation of souls in *any way* she could, and that is the essence of the Little Way: an openness to suffer anything, no matter how big or small, in order to participate in Christ's redemptive work.

Thérèse desired to follow this way so fiercely, that she would often tell Jesus that He had already suffered enough during His thirty-three years on earth, that it was time for Him to rest, and let it be her turn to fight and to suffer.[3] Also keep in mind that she was not trying to kill herself, though she always longed for Heaven. During her illness, she had many visits from a doctor and accepted any medical attempts that were made to treat her. If her situation had been treatable and she could have survived, I believe she would have, but she knew she was dying and so she let herself suffer with abandon in order to do as much good for souls as she could prior to her passing. She was a hero.

So with that, Thérèse got her "greatest opportunities" to suffer for Jesus and for participating in His redemption of souls with the onset of her tuberculosis, and was diligent in taking advantage of any opening given to her. When she first coughed up blood on Good Friday of 1896, she made it a point to carry out her duties, which involved exhausting physical labor, and to observe the Lenten fastings, which include only eating dry bread and drinking only water, for as long as she could, even though her physical strength was weakening from the start. Thérèse only told two people about her illness at first: the Sister who was in charge of the infirmary, who was sworn to silence, and her Prioress, Mother Marie de Gonzague, who at Thérèse's request, gave her permission to carry on as usual.

The infirmarian at the time, who had been one of Thérèse's novices, Sister Marie of the Trinity and the Holy Face, begged the Mother Prioress to revoke that "insane permission" and order Thérèse to rest. Mother Marie de Gonzague refused, saying that Thérèse could come and request that herself if she felt the need. That Good Friday, Marie of the Trinity spotted Thérèse climbing a ladder to wash windows, looking pale and fatigued. Marie of the Trinity begged her to come down and let her finish the task for her. Thérèse refused, insisting that she could bear a slight fatigue for Jesus on the day (Good Friday) in which He had suffered so much for her. When Thérèse learned that Marie of the Trinity had been pleading for her to the Mother Prioress, she begged her not to again, insisting that the prioress was being inspired by Jesus to allow Thérèse to carry on to the end of her strength.[4]

---

[3] *Thérèse and Marie of the Trinity* pg. 104
[4] Ibid. pg. 101-103

Walking was extremely taxing for Thérèse as her condition continued to worsen. She was told, however, by another infirmarian that a 30 minute walk every day would do her some good. Her oldest blood sister, Sister Marie of the Sacred Heart, saw how Thérèse was struggling and advised her to stop, saying that the walking was exhausting her and not really doing her any good. Thérèse responded, "It's true, but you know what gives me strength? Well, I am walking for a missionary. I think that over there, far away, one of them is perhaps exhausted in his apostolic endeavours, and, to lessen his fatigue, I offer mine to God."[5] That is one of the clearest examples of how the Little Way works, in which Thérèse takes something seemingly insignificant and potentially even harmful, and offers it to God to bring good out of it for someone else. In fact, somehow it was later confirmed that *at the same time* she was "walking for a missionary," there was actually a missionary priest of the Oblates of Mary Immaculate, by the name of Father Breynat, trying to make what felt like an impossible trek in the North American Arctic and, without knowing how, found the strength to complete it! He later became a bishop.[6]

Eventually, as her illness continued to worsen, Thérèse was relieved of her duties. Her blood sisters were assigned to look after her. Also, due to Marie of the Trinity's youth, she was relieved of infirmarian duties for fear that she might catch Thérèse's tuberculosis and also ordered to stay away from Thérèse altogether. This was crushing for Marie of the Trinity who had grown very close to Thérèse, having been her novice and really having come to regard Thérèse as her best friend and as a mother to her despite their closeness in age. Overtime, Thérèse began to require assistance for getting around; again walking became more and more difficult for her. By the time she died, in fact, she only had half a lung to breathe with.

One day, however, Thérèse had been carted into the garden and left alone to have fresh air outside. Marie of the Trinity was taking a walk, deeply depressed from the three months of reports of Thérèse's continuing decline topped with the inability to see her. As she was walking, she spotted Thérèse sitting in her wheelchair. Thérèse saw her as well and motioned for Marie of the Trinity to come over to her. Marie responded "Oh no!

---

[5] *Her Last Conversations* pg. 262

[6] Reverend Thomas Cook, *The Vision of Priesthood in the Writings of Saint Thérèse of Lisieux*, 1998.

We will be seen and I don't have permission!" She then ran away into a grotto, fell to her knees, and began weeping. With surprise she looked up to see Thérèse sitting on a stump beside her. Thérèse said "I have not been forbidden to come to you, and even though I should die of it, I want to console you." Thérèse then embraced her and dried her tears. Marie of the Trinity, seeing how Thérèse was trembling with fever begged her to return to her wheelchair. Thérèse responded, "Yes, but not before you have laughed for me." Marie of the Trinity quickly obeyed.[7]

When Thérèse was permanently moved into the infirmary, even there she found ways to give of herself for the sake of souls. When told to drink some water, she would want to refuse because her mouth was not feeling dry, but was reminded that out of obedience she was to accept any treatment or nourishment presented to her, and so she would. At least one time, late at night, one of her sisters gave her water and then fell asleep while Thérèse was still holding the cup in her hands. Thérèse did not wake her, and the sister would wake up horrified to find Thérèse still holding the cup, her hands shaking. This kind of echoes something that Thérèse endured in her early years in Carmel. One of the Sisters was helping her fasten her scapular, which is fastened at the shoulder by a large pin. The Sister accidently ran it through Thérèse's skin. Thérèse joyfully endured the pain in silence for several hours![8] I would imagine, Thérèse may have reflected on this while undergoing an extremely painful treatment called "pointes de feu", which means "points of fire." It was a cauterizing remedy for tuberculosis used during her time in which red-hot needles were plunged into the flesh. Her sister Celine counted 500 marks on Thérèse's back from "pointes de feu."[9]

Her condition of tuberculosis brought other complications besides slowly suffocating her and causing her to cough up blood. She endured terrible digestive issues, including gangrene in her intestines. When she learned about her gangrene issue, her response was "Well, all the better!"[10] Thérèse did verbally express her physical agony on occasion, saying that she never would have believed it was possible to suffer so much, and also saying that if she did not have faith she would have killed herself without a second

---

[7] Ibid. pg. 265
[8] *My Sister Saint Thérèse* pg. 187
[9] *St. Thérèse: Doctor of the Little Way* pg. 93
[10] *Story of a Soul* 3rd Edition pg. 264

of hesitation; yet she always maintained that she was at peace, and this was a peace that persisted even in the face of a great spiritual darkness that she was enduring, what is called the dark night of the soul or the night of faith.

To put it simply, the dark night of the soul is a stage that one can reach in his or her life with God where all perceptible spiritual consolation is removed. Thérèse entered this state two days after she first coughed up blood, on Easter Sunday of 1896. She remained in this state until her death, September 30, 1897. This demonstrates a whole new level of heroism in her. We can tend to wonder how atheists give their life meaning without the hope of an eternal tomorrow. We as Christians can think, "Oh, I can suffer anything because I have God to comfort me."

Thérèse had *no* spiritual comfort in the agony of her illness. She felt mocked in her hope for Heaven. It's not that she feared she would not get there, it was that she felt like it was not there to get to, and that all that awaited her was the dark night of nothingness. Even in this darkness, however, she would write poems expressing her love and zeal for God. She even wrote out the Creed in her own blood. Her fellow Carmelites continuously expressed what an encouragement she was and what "spiritual lights and consolations" she must be receiving in order to endure her physical suffering so well. She did at times talk of the darkness she was enduring, and after doing so she ventured that she must have seemed to be exaggerating her trial given how encouragingly she spoke of her faith, but her response to any suggestions that she had almost transcended the veil of faith, was that it was not a veil, but a wall. She felt absolutely no joy in discussing the happiness of Heaven and the eternal possession of God; on the contrary, it was a source of struggle and torment for her, but she said "I simply sing what I want to believe."

Her will to hold on to her faith was fostered by a selfless love toward God that she had been disposing herself to her whole life. All she ever wanted in her love for Him was to bring pleasure to Him, whether or not she got anything back for it, and whether or not HE even knew it was from her. She referred to herself as a little ball for the Child Jesus to hold to His Heart, throw against a wall, or simply ignore and go to sleep next to. All that mattered to Thérèse was that she loved God, and not whether she felt any consolation in return. Thérèse has a quote from Saint John of the Cross written in French on the coat of arms she designed that says "Love is repaid by love alone." That was her motto. She lived for love and wanted to die of love.

The day Thérèse died, she was physically and spiritually battered. She was breathing through half a lung, her hands were blue, she was unhealthily thin, and she appeared much older than her years. Before she died, however, she suddenly sat up in her bed, her eyes wide and a radiance coming over her face. She looked at her crucifix and said "Oh! I love Him...My God...I love you!..." Her head fell back, but she remained sitting up, her eyes fixed on a spot above a statue of Mary that she had. She held this position for the amount of time it would take to say the Creed, then she collapsed with her eyes closed, a very beautiful and youthful look on her face, and the hint of a mysterious smile.[11] There are many pictures that were taken of Thérèse, but I find the picture of her after she died to be the most beautiful. There is a peacefulness on her face, that I believe is a testament to the unspeakable tenderness of God.

III. Doctor of the Church?

I will not presume to speak for the Catholic Church as to why Thérèse was proclaimed a Doctor of the Church, so I will let the Church speak for herself through the quotes I have compiled below from Thérèse's canonization and doctrinization.

Before I do, however, one might ask: what is a Doctor of the Church? Pope Saint John Paul II puts it nicely in the very homily in which he decrees Thérèse's doctoralship: "Indeed, when the Magisterium proclaims someone a doctor of the Church, it intends to point out to all the faithful, particularly to those who perform in the Church the fundamental service of preaching or who undertake the delicate task of theological teaching and research, that the doctrine professed and proclaimed by a certain person can be a reference point, not only because it conforms to revealed truth, but also because it sheds new light on the mysteries of the faith, a deeper understanding of Christ's mystery." (See third document below)

---

[11] *Therese and Lisieux* pg. 308

Homily of Pope Pius XI at the Canonization of St. Thérèse on 17 May 1925 and *Bull of Canonization of St. Thérèse of the Child Jesus and the Holy Face.* (**Vehementer exultamus hodie**)

"If the way of spiritual childhood became general, who does not see how easily would be realized the reformation of human society..."[12]

"...the peculiar characteristic of the sanctity to which God called Thérèse of the Child Jesus lies chiefly in this, that having heard the Divine call, she obeyed with the utmost promptness and fidelity. Without going beyond the common order of things, in her way of life she followed out and fulfilled her vocation with such alacrity, generosity, and constancy that she reached an heroic degree of virtue. In our own day, when men seek so passionately after temporal goods, this young maiden lived in our midst practicing in all simplicity and devotedness the Christian virtues in order to honor God and to win eternal life. May her example strengthen in virtue and lead to a more perfect life, not only the cloistered souls but those living in the world."[13]

APOSTOLIC LETTER OF HIS HOLINESS POPE JOHN PAUL II
DIVINI AMORIS SCIENTIA
SAINT THÉRÈSE OF THE CHILD JESUS AND
THE HOLY FACE IS PROCLAIMED A DOCTOR
OF THE UNIVERSAL CHURCH

"Through spiritual childhood one experiences that everything comes from God, returns to him and abides in him, for the salvation of all, in a mystery of merciful love. Such is the doctrinal message taught and lived by this Saint." (nn. 8)

---

[12] In other words, the pope is saying that if everyone followed the Little Way, the wounds of our civilization would be healed. To put it even simpler, Thérèse's Little Way has the capacity to save the world.

[13] The pope is in essence proclaiming that Thérèse is for all and that her Little Way is accessible to all no matter their state in life.

111

"Her writings contain over 1,000 biblical quotations: more than 400 from the Old Testament and over 600 from the New." (nn. 9)[14]

"A sign of the ecclesial reception of the Saint's teaching is the appeal to her doctrine in many documents of the Church's ordinary Magisterium, especially when speaking of the contemplative and missionary vocation,[15] of trust in the just and merciful God, of Christian joy and of the call to holiness. Evidence of this fact is the presence of her doctrine in the recent Catechism of the Catholic Church (nn. 127[the New Testament], 826 [the Church's holiness], 956 [Church relations between Heaven and Earth][16], 1011 [the meaning of Christian death], 2011 [Merit], 2558 [What is Prayer? 'For me, prayer is a surge of the heart; it is a simple look turned toward heaven, it is a cry of recognition and of love, embracing both trial and joy.' *Story of a Soul* pg. 242. Sadly, the *Catechism of the Catholic Church* does not finish her sentence. She concludes '…finally, it is something great, supernatural, which expands my soul and unites me to Jesus.'---JDW]).[17] She who so loved to learn the truths of the faith, in the catechism deserved to be included among the authoritative witnesses of Catholic doctrine." (nn. 10)

"…Thérèse of Lisieux is a *young person*. She reached the maturity of holiness in the prime of youth (cf. *Ms C,* 4r). As such, she appears as a

---

[14] This gives a glimpse of how profound a scholarship Thérèse possessed, though she was not extensively educated.

[15] It is interesting how JPII phrases that, as if contemplative and missionary are merely specific vocations of the Church to which more can be added. I see contemplative and missionary as opposite extremes. Thérèse being relevant for both of these vocations, means that she is relevant for *all* vocations. In essence, there is not a single Catholic who should not be familiar with Thérèse and her Little Way.

[16] This eludes to one of the most unique doctrines of our Catholic faith: the fact that we can spend our heaven doing good on earth.

[17] *CCC's* use of Thérèse as an authority on prayer is the most profound. *CCC* literally asks "What is prayer?" and then right below that it cites Thérèse's quote on it and then *CCC* simply moves on to another section without any further comment. This implies that in our day, Thérèse, this dead at 24, uneducated nun, is *THE* authority on prayer in the Catholic Tradition outside of Scripture.

Teacher of evangelical life, particularly effective in illumining the paths of young people, who must be the leaders and witnesses of the Gospel to the new generations." (nn. 11)

"Thérèse is a Teacher for our time, which thirsts for living and essential words, for heroic and credible acts of witness. For this reason she is also loved and accepted by brothers and sisters of other Christian communities and even by non-Christians." (ibid.)[18]

PROCLAMATION OF ST THÉRÈSE OF THE CHILD JESUS AND THE HOLY FACE AS A "DOCTOR OF THE CHURCH" *HOMILY OF POPE JOHN PAUL II* *Sunday, 19 October 1997*

"She was one, to the point that she could be proclaimed patroness of the missions. Jesus himself showed her how she could live this vocation: by fully practising the commandment of love, she would be immersed in the very heart of the Church's mission, supporting those who proclaim the Gospel with the mysterious power of prayer and communion. Thus she achieved what the Second Vatican Council emphasized in teaching that the Church is missionary by nature (cf. Ad gentes, n. 2). Not only those who choose the missionary life but all the baptized are in some way sent ad gentes." (nn. 2)

"Charity", she wrote, "gave me the key to my vocation. I understood that if the Church had a body composed of different members, the most necessary and most noble of all could not be lacking to it, and so I understood that the Church had a heart and that this heart was burning with love. I understood that it was love alone that made the Church's members act, that if love were ever extinguished, apostles would not proclaim the Gospel and martyrs would refuse to shed their blood. I understood that love includes all vocations.... Then in the excess of my

---

[18] Thérèse really is for *EVERYONE*.

delirious joy, I cried out: "O Jesus, my Love... at last I have found my vocation; my vocation is Love!'" (nn. 4).

"Thérèse of Lisieux did not only grasp and describe the profound truth of Love as the centre and heart of the Church, but in her short life she lived it intensely. It is precisely this convergence of doctrine and concrete experience, of truth and life, of teaching and practice, which shines with *particular* brightness in this saint, and which makes her an attractive model especially for young people and *for those who are seeking true meaning for their life*." (nn. 5)[19]

"She counters a rational culture, so often overcome by practical materialism, with the disarming simplicity of *the "little way"* which, by returning to the essentials, *leads to the secret of all life*:[20] the divine Love that surrounds and penetrates every human venture. In a time like ours, so frequently marked by an ephemeral and hedonistic culture, this new doctor of the Church proves to be remarkably effective in enlightening the mind and heart of those who hunger and thirst for truth and love." (ibid.)

"The way she took to reach this ideal of life is not that of the great undertakings reserved for the few, but on the contrary, a way within everyone's reach, the "little way", a path of trust and total self-abandonment to the Lord's grace. It is not a prosaic way, as if it were less demanding. It is in fact a demanding reality, as the Gospel always is. But it is a way in which one is imbued with a sense of trusting abandonment to divine mercy, which makes even the most rigorous spiritual commitment light. Because of this way in which she receives everything as 'grace', because she puts her relationship with Christ and her choice of love at the centre of everything, because of the place she gives to the ardent impulses of the heart on her spiritual journey, Thérèse of Lisieux is a saint who remains young despite the passing years, and she is held up as an eminent model and guide on the path of Christians, as we approach the third millennium." (nn. 6)[21]

---

[19] Very powerful. Italics are mine.
[20] Also very powerful. Italics are mine.
[21] In other words, she is *The Modern Times Saint* (original title of *The Smallest Spark*).

IV. Conclusion

Thérèse's potential value to the life of any person of good will really cannot be exhausted or sufficiently explained. She has to be experienced on an individual level and allowed to speak for herself, especially in *Story of a Soul, Her Last Conversations,* and *My Sister Saint Thérèse.* I have generally seen a tendency in which people view her in a childish light that misses out on the spiritual steel which was in her heart and how good a friend she can be in one's own walk with God and through life. It is true that she did those things for which she has been stereotyped, such as throwing flowers at crucifixes or other holy images, and other things that can appear saccharine; but if everyone were to know the other side of Thérèse and embrace her as a whole person, while following her example of courage and continual self-gift, who is to say, as Pope Pius XI speculated, that the wounds of our society would not indeed be healed, especially the wounds of war and poverty?

Saint Thérèse of Lisieux: Pray for Us!

Appendix II

References:

Initial reaction to first cough---*Thérèse and Marie of the Trinity* pg. 101-103
What Thérèse does when she gets up in the morning and her statement on
    courage---Ibid. pg. 104
Thérèse singing what she wants---Ibid. pg. 33
Life is not sad!---Ibid. pg. xix-xx
Thérèse walking for missionaries---*Her Last Conversations* pg. 262
My favorite story---Ibid. pg. 265
Thérèse on Heaven---Ibid. pg. 102
A small spark---Ibid. pg. 99
What Celine is to say in response to Thérèse's suffering---*My Sister Saint*
    Thérèse pg. 234
Thérèse on eating---Ibid. pg. 167
Thérèse's freedom---Ibid. pg. 178
Thérèse and the pin---Ibid. pg. 187
A verse of poetry---Ibid. pg. 86-87
The parable of the rabbit---Ibid. pg. 59
Thérèse's reflection on her dark night---*The Passion of Thérèse of Lisieux*
    pg. 55-57
Thérèse's medical examination---Ibid. pg. 39-40
Thérèse's efforts to talk despite suffocation---Ibid. pg. 100
Thérèse's emanciation---Ibid. pg 101
Thérèse on interior suffering---Ibid. pg. 103
Thérèse unable to receive Communion and her sisters fear her despair---
    Ibid. pg. 118-121

Thérèse's most beautiful picture---*Therese* (sic.) *and Lisieux* pg. 308
Thérèse on prayer---*Story of a Soul* 3rd Edition pg. 242
Thérèse faced with gangrene---Ibid. 264
Thérèse's death---*Story of a Soul* 3rd Edition pg. 269-271
Her Last Conversations pg. 205-207
My Sister Saint Thérèse pg. 238-246
Therese (sic.) and Lisieux pg. 306

About the Author

Like Thérèse, John D. Wright is an ordinary person who has never been looking to make a name for himself. Since reading Thérèse's autobiography in 2009, he has immersed himself in her literature while also engaging seminary studies.

A native millennial of Savannah, Georgia, who majored in Criminal Justice at the University of Georgia and enjoys video games, movies, martial arts, roller coasters, and laser tag, John stands as a perfect example of a seemingly random person who has joined a host of others in feeling great affection for an obscure young woman who lived and died in the late nineteenth century.

Printed in the United States
By Bookmasters